Sex & Attention III

Ordering Information:
Quantity sales. Special discounts are available on quantity
purchases by corporations, associations, and others. For
details, contact the publisher at the website or email above.

Printed in the United States of America

Sex & Attention III
Series: Sex & Attention

ISBN-13:

Dedication

This book is dedicated to the Aquarius in my life. You all were my air when I was suffocating. To my Aquarius bestie, Aquarius daughter, and the Aquarius rising who helped me create her ... thank you for not giving up on me even when things were challenging. I love you with every fiber of my being.

Books by Sasha Owens

Voices Unveiled

Voices Continued

Sex & Attention

Sex & Attention II

Sex & Attention III

Spotted

Sex & Attention III

Contents

Prologue

So as promised I told you that I would give you the story of Lamont. Lamont Ivy. Lamont is the guy that started it all. Lamont was my 1st love and for a while he was my only love. I prepped myself as a young woman and I knew that I would marry Lamont. He was perfect. He helped me grow into a classy, young lady. When I was with Lamont I felt like a beautiful rose. I felt that with every kiss and every touch from him I bloomed into something even more exquisite. When I thought of love, I thought of Lamont. There wasn't anything he could do wrong to me because his love felt so pure. It felt real and it made me feel human. Lamont's love healed my scars and later it helped form other scars. However, I never questioned if Lamont's love for me was real. It had to be. When I thought of my wedding day, I saw his face. When I thought of my future children, I saw his face. When I thought of having a new set of parents, I saw his parents. Every moment led up to him. Well that was before there was a Kich and a Zay. Now we're at the third part of my story and I have split my heart 3 ways. These men will not share me. So, who do I choose? This is my final choice and when I lay everything on the line who is worth it? Who has true power over my heart. True love is unconditional.

Which means I love you for you. I love you regardless of the things you've done and regardless of the trash you bring. Who will I...Vistoria Jefferson whisk away into the sunlight of my beautiful darkness with?

Chapter 1
<u>Papa</u>

"Papa," I said as I jumped in his lap.

"Goodness, Vistoria you're getting so big," he said as he wrapped his arms around me.

Papa was my grandfather and I was definitely a grandfather's girl. I would run pass my mom and my dad just to get to him my entire life.

"Stori, aren't you too big to be jumping in his lap like that," my mom said.

"Nope, Papa is a big man and he can take it," I said as I squeezed his cheeks and kissed him on the nose.

My Papa was a big, strong black man. He was 6'5" with broad shoulders and around 280 pounds. So with me weighing only like 130 then he definitely had no issues with me sitting in his lap.

"You worry about yourself Pene," Papa said to my mom.

My mom's name was Penelope but grandpa called her Pene for short. He said she was small and copper like a fresh penny.

I squirmed and smiled at my Papa. He tapped me on my nose.

"My Tori, Stori," he said as he tickled me.

"Papa no, stop. You know I hate being tickled," I said.

"So I hear you got some big headed boy coming over for dinner tonight," he said.

I sat up straight and tried to look mature.

"Yea I wanted to know if it was ok to invite my friend Lamont over," I said.

"Friend? And what kind of friend is this boy Stori?" he asked.

I looked up at my mom for some help.

"Well Dad, he's…..," she started to say but Papa cut her off.

"No, Pene. I want to hear her say it from her mouth. If she's old enough to invite boys over she surely must be old enough to tell me what's their relations together," he said.

"He's my boyfriend," I said embarrassed.

"Dad….," Mom tried to intervene.

"You're only 17 years old Stori. What do you know about having a boyfriend?" he asked.

"I'll be 18 at the end of this year. That's grown," I said as I tried to muster up some confidence.

"I'll be legal and I can do things," I continued.

"Things?" Papa made a face.

"Dad…leave that girl alone. If me and her dad have met him and we don't have a problem then neither should you," she said.

I looked at mom and then I looked at Papa to see if he was falling for it.

"You're right. I guess I still look in these eyes and see my baby girl. And I didn't realize my baby girl is becoming a woman. I gotta respect that. I look forward to meeting your boyfriend. Because I trust that I've raised you to pick a charitable suitor. One with much dignity and valor," he continued.

"Oh Stori, you've gotten him started. He's in monologue phase," Mom teased as she exited the room throwing her hands in the air.

"I can't wait to meet this young man. If he's good enough for my Stori then he's good enough for me," Papa said.

My eyes opened and I was soaked in sweat. I looked over and there was Kich…still sleeping.

Because I trust that I've raised you to pick a charitable suitor. One with much dignity and valor.

I looked over at my sleeping sadist and I wondered would he had been a charitable suitor for my grandpa.

He's giving, he's brave, he loves me with all his soul.

Yea and you also share him with other women. One who doesn't like you all that well at the moment.

I threw my legs off the side of the bed and placed them into my house shoes. I flung my robe on and dropped my cell phone in the pocket. The moment my foot hit the floor Kich was up rubbing my back.

"Is something wrong Princess?" he asked.

"No, I just need to go get a drink of water. My mouth is really dry," I said.

"Should I hire a full-time maid so you won't have to get up in the night like this? I could have a day shift one and one on night shift. Or a butler maybe if you promise not to fuck him," he said.

"No that's not necessary. I don't mind going to get my water and it gives me some time to breath while I'm walking," I said.

"But I need you here with me in every moment. I hate waking up and you're not next to me," he said.

"It's only for a second. I just have a lot on my mind....ya know," I said.

"You've been having a lot of bad dreams lately," he said.

That's because I've been keeping it from you that my ex is trying to win me back.

"Yea I have," I said as I looked down in guilt.

"Was the move too much? Should we have waited? I know you and Mel had your problems in the past but it seems like you're really starting to come together as a family," he said.

"Yea we are. Kich it's not anything you've done. I promise," I reassured.

"Moments like this I wish I was omniscient," he laughed.

"Can I go get my water now?" I asked.

"Yes, but hurry back to me," he said.

I quickly exited the room so I could go get my water. Which I wasn't even that thirsty. I wanted to text Lamont.

I got in the kitchen and I rummaged through the cabinet to get a glass with my left hand. I dug my phone from my robe with my right hand. I went to my messages and I opened up Lamont's.

Lamont

Book I did this
all for you.

You didn't do
it for me.

Every night I
had to sleep in
a bed that didn't
have you in it was
torture. I felt like
I was dying.

That was your
choice. And now
you expect me to
feel sorry for you.
If slavery was
a choice, then your
crappy ass marriage
was one.
You expect

me

to drop everything
I have going right
now for you.
It's not fair.
You're still selfish.
You don't care about
me. You want what
you want and to hell with
what Vistoria wants.

Book, come on
it's not like that.
I'm in love with
you.
       I hit the phone icon in rage.

          ***Calling Lamont**

           "Hello."

        "Who in the fuck do you

think you are? Huh?"

I whispered in the phone but made sure
I added emphasis so he could feel my anger.

"Book I'm not tryna upset you."
"Stop. Stop now.
Do not call me Book.
My name is Vistoria.
I don't want your little pet name.
I don't want to think about
your fucking analogy.
Ohh, you're more than just a Stori
to me you're my whole Book."

I said as I made mimicking sounds and
rolling my eyes.

"You're a joke.
A bad one at that.
You really think I'm going to stop
and end everything for you.
You want unconditional love
when you have only given me shit."

"You're so upset Book…
Vistoria because you still feel it.
How many men did you go through
in search for me?
How many men did you
leave by the wayside

because they didn't fulfill it?
Tell me."

"I don't have to tell you anything.
It's none of your business."

"And now you're dating
some guy that dates you
and other women. Wow."

"You don't get to
fucking judge my life.
And at least he's honest.
Something you know nothing about.
See you tell me we're in a monogamist
relationship meanwhile you're out giving all
my love to someone else.
Then you leave me for her.
And then you marry her.
Cause see that's what kinda guy you are. You
say he wants his cake and to eat it too.
You're no different.
You're just a liar wrapped
in monogamy paper."

"Your grandfather loved me
and that's not something
you can say about this cat."

"Bye. You bastard.

Fuck you Lamont."

I ended the call and headed for the sink to throw some water on my face.

"Hey, I didn't see you standing there," I said.

"Yea I know. If you had you probably wouldn't have had that conversation while I was listening," said Melanie.

"It's not a big deal," I said.

"Are you sure. You seem a little upset. Should we go get Kich?" she asked as she pointed upstairs.

"Don't," I said and pulled her hand down and looked viciously into her eyes.

"You know his rules and it seems like you're up to something. If you hurt him," she said as she snatched her hand back.

"I will personally deliver the ass whooping to you," she said as she exited the kitchen.

"Why do you hate me?" I asked.

"What did I do to you?" I began crying.

"Seriously, you're gonna cry?" she turned around.

"I didn't ask for this. I knew nothing about what I was signing up for the day I met him. All of this was thrown on me," I said.

"Oh bullshit. You knew soon enough to make a decision not to choose him. You want to play so innocent Stori. You want to act as if life has been thrown at you, but you're present and you've chosen every moment. You're such a fucking child, grow the fuck up," she stepped to me and then Kich flicked the lights on.

"What is going on in here?" he looked back and forth between us.

I just turned and walked out.

"You can tell him whatever you want. I don't even care anymore," I said as I began exiting the kitchen.

"Are you going to get your water?" Kich asked.

I turned around and grabbed it then I headed back upstairs.

The house was freezing because Kich loved it that way. I quickly rushed up the steps and got in the bed. I pulled up the cover over my head and sunk deep into the clouds of pillows on the bed.

Your grandfather loved me and that's not something you can say about this cat.

The thought played in my head as I was dosing back off. Memories of that moment my Papa met Lamont came rushing back. Memories of the moments that occurred after came flooding in also.

"I'm gone marry your granddaughter one day," Lamont said to Papa as we sat at the dinner table.

"You know that's how it use to be done. We didn't play games when we found us a good woman," Papa said.

"I love Stori and I know I want to be with her," Lamont said.

"Well Stori you have to at least reach 18 before you consider being someone's wife and it wouldn't hurt if you learned to clean up more," my mom said.

"Pene," Papa corrected her.

"What? I was just telling the truth and the truth shall...," Papa cut her off.

"...Make you shut yo' damn mouth and stop embarrassing my baby girl," he said firmly.

"I don't see anything wrong with the young man making it known that he wants her hand in marriage that's what respectable men do. Especially one that's...how old are you son?" he asked Lamont.

"I'm 19," he said.

"Nineteen is a good age. Why I was a little older than that when I asked for your mother's hand in marriage. I waited for her to turn 18, but that's just how things were done back in my day," he said.

I laughed a little before the darker memories started to flood my mental... strangling my happiness.

I sat outside the church crying that day and contemplating going in. I was in my all black dress and for emphasis I even added an all-black lip. I wanted my outside appearance to resemble how broken I truly was on the inside. I sat in my coupe and grimaced at the morning sun.

Why the fuck is the sun shining all happy? This isn't a happy moment. I'm burying my Papa today and God has the audacity to make today pretty.

I had hoped for rain...a car-flipping hurricane type rain because maybe then someone could understand what I was going through.

As I continued to daze into my bliss I was startled by a knock to my window. I looked out and it was Lamont. Normally I lit up with heart eyes and sparkles after gazing at him but not this day. This day I looked into his eyes and sought out his soul and hoped it was as black as mine.

I slowly moved my finger over the button to let the window down.

"Bookie, you ready?" he asked.

"What am I getting ready for exactly? Congratulating God for taking my grandfather away? Great job," I snarled.

"We all belong to God and He is gracious enough to gift us with each other but for a time. Your grandfather fought as long as he could, but the cancer took control. You are blessed. You got to say goodbye. It wasn't an abrupt loss," Lamont said.

"I got to say goodbye?…I got to watch him die," I allowed the words to flow from my mouth very slowly so he could feel it.

Lamont reached his hands in the car and unlocked the door.

"Come on, you don't know it yet, but you'll be in more pain if you miss his funeral," he easily scooped me up and pulled me close to his side. I pulled my black sunglasses from my bag because I didn't want to look into anyone's eyes and I didn't want them looking into mine.

As we sat there on the front pew I watched as the competition started. It seemed the extra people in the family were happy for an audience where they could see who cried the loudest. One of my aunts cradled the casket ,but she was also the one who hadn't visited him in years. Those tears were probably there after she realized he hadn't left her any money.

I pretty much tossed and turned all night with the ghosts of my past.

Forbidden Love

How did you become
my forbidden love?
My forbidden fruit.
It's like the more we become entangled
the more I thought of you...
We meet in my dreams.
I can't keep you away.
But I couldn't own your love.
I know you'd never stay.

I woke up the next morning and I had an ache in my chest. I stared at the ceiling and I let time past for a moment. I finally pushed pass my emotions and slipped on my robe and house shoes to head for the kitchen.

Once I got in the kitchen I grabbed a bag of frozen strawberries, a banana, chia seeds, and peaches to make a smoothie. I must've been totally out of it because I didn't realize Melanie was sitting off in a corner looking out of the window.

"Hey," I said.

"What's up," Melanie responded.

"Look I'm sorry about last night," I said.

"It happens. Families argue," she said.

"I shouldn't have screamed at you. It wasn't you that I was angry at and I shouldn't have given you my poison," she said.

"So did you ever tell Kich about what really had you upset?" she asked.

"No, didn't you?" I asked.

"That's not my call. He wouldn't believe me anyways. Cause see Kich believes that you're totally honest with him and that you wouldn't keep anything from him," she said.

"Yea, I don't want to hurt him," I said.

"What hurts Kich more is a liar. Because he's so open. I won't lie. I didn't tell him for a few reasons. I know that if it comes out later I won't be the only one he sees as broken. I won't be the only one who's lost his trust," she continued.

"Melanie, he trusts you with everything. He trusts you with things that could destroy him. Do you not see your worth?" I asked.

"He loves you more," she said.

"He loves us differently, but it's still love. I'm the one new to the poly-life. He's trying to make us a family, but we are making it hard," I said and I walked over to her.

"You bring out something in him. You know him. And I don't know the full story of how you guys met but I do know it must have been life-changing. He says you freed him," I said.

"That's a story…best told by Kich. He'll tell you when he's ready. Although I know it verbatim it's always better from his mouth," she said as she walked closer to me.

I could feel my hair on my body stand up and throat tighten. Melanie was sexy. She was porn star sexy and she fucked like one.

"Come here," I said as I pulled her face in and started kissing her.

"This is what we should be doing instead of fighting all the time," she said.

I licked my finger and then I stuck it between the lining of her shorts. She never wore panties so I was smooth sailing. I started rubbing on her clit and then I worked my way down to her opening. I pushed her back on the kitchen counter.

"Take these shorts off," I demanded as I unbuttoned the top for her.

She quickly slid out of them and I just looked at her plump pussy that was already secreting. I slurped it all up.

At that moment Kich walked in the house and my face was buried in her vagina.

"I see you two are finally getting along. Good," he hung his keys up and exited.

I lifted my head and just laughed.

Chapter 2

Trouble in Paradise

"Correct me if I'm wrong but weren't you just face down, ass up eating her out?" Kich joked.

"Uhhh, she's a fucking bitch and she's annoying as hell," I groaned as I peeled off the paper to my sour cream and onion chip can.

"You're so flip-flop. You can't act like you hate her every time the day doesn't go how Vistoria wants it. You're spoiled and entitled," Kich said.

"She's spiteful and a Cancer," I said.

"Here we go with your astro talk," Kich exhaled.

"Yep and we're gonna keep going. She needs to let me do her chart," I complained.

"Vistoria you do realize no one has to give you their information so you can type it in and try to learn every thing about them from past lives to the future," Kich said.

"Well she claims she doesn't believe in all that astrology stuff," I said.

"It still isn't groun....," I cut Kich off.

"Which is a lie because she believes in brujere. It's all occultic as they say," I sat down in the living room and propped my foot on the ottoman in front of me.

"I don't get why they classify being spiritual in a different form occultic but oh well," she still participates in it.

"She doesn't want to bond on anything that interest me because she hates me," I sighed.

"You have to understand. Melanie hasn't had to live with another woman in a long time. Especially one she knows I adore as much as I do you," Kich said.

"I didn't think it would be like this," I said.

"How did you think it would be?" he asked.

"Don't you have siblings or cousins?" he continued.

"Well yeah," I said as he cut me off.

"Ok then. You should understand. You can like or love a person, but you must expect boundaries of any relationship to be tested when a new piece comes into the game," he said.

"But I'm not a new piece. I've been here for two years now," I griped.

"Oh Vistoria, you are very new. You have barely scraped the surface," he said.

"Visiting and living with someone are two different things," he said.

"Who do you like fucking more?" I asked.

"What?" he asked.

"You heard me. Who do you like fucking more? Me or Melanie?" I asked.

"We're discussing the cat fight y'all just had and you want to know who I like fucking more?" he continued.

"Yes, I want to know," he said.

"That question is irrelevant because I don't compare," he said.

"Bullshit," I said.

"Watch your tone Vistoria," he replied.

"Last night you stayed in her longer than you did me," I said.

"Are you timing me now?" he asked.

"Yes," I said.

"Well don't. I'm here to please both of you. It wouldn't be fair to you if I pulled out right when you were about to cum," he said.

I looked away. He pulled my face back to look at him.

"Would you like that?" he asked.

"I suppose I wouldn't," I said.

"You think you have it hard Vistoria? You're a spoiled, fucking brat. Melanie is probably sick at the thought of you, but she knows she can't do anything about it if she wants me. I fucking love the air you breath and the ground you walk upon. I'm the Dom but I would serve you with my fucking life. Yes, this is my lifestyle. I love sex. I love fucking. I'm a nymphomaniac. But all of that means shit if I can't have you. Until I met you all this seemed to just be a fix to keep my cravings at bay but you Vistoria. You are my antidote," Kich said.

I swallowed my chip really hard. *Gulp.* My brain was juggling all that Kich just said and trying to swallow so chaos was inevitable. My chip went down the wrong way and instead of me looking at Kich googly eyed I was now gasping for air with water streaming from the crevices of my eyes.

Of course Kich ran over like a concerned parent performing CPR on me.

"I'm.....O......K.....," I said in between Kich's thrust to my abdomen.

"Mel can you bring me a glass of water?" Kich yelled.

I straightened up in my seat as I continuously cleared my throat. "I believe she was upstairs so I'm sure she didn't hear you. I'll go..." I stopped as Mel interrupted me.

"Here you go Daddy," Mel was holding a slender, clear glass filled with water.

"Alkaline just how you prefer," she handed the glass to Kich and Kich handed it to me.

For a moment, I felt it. I felt the envy Mel must've felt when dealing with me. I hesitated to drink out of embarrassment. I couldn't look her in her eyes.

What was I doing there? I could be with Lamont living a normal life. Why am I here?

Stop it. This is what Lamont wants. He's poisoning you and making you want to get back with him. He married another woman on you.

Yeah and Kich dates other women in your face.

Lamont is a liar. Kich tells the truth.

"Vistoria is that better," Kich was sitting up firmly and peering into my soul.

I backed away a little.

"Yes," I answered. Sometimes when I looked into Kich's deep, dark eyes I felt like I was drowning.

"Can I be excused?" I asked.

Mel shriveled the corner of her eye and tightened her mouth...it was like she could read my thoughts. It was like she sensed my disconnect.

Was I disconnecting?

"Yes you may be excused," Kich answered.

I picked up my empty glass, pushed my feet into my slippers, and scurried out. I wanted to be alone. All alone.

I started to make my way up the stairs when I felt Kich grab my hand. I turned around to see his silhouette cradled on the steps.

"Who is he?" Kich asked.

"Kich what do you mean?" I snarled as I wondered if Mel had ratted me out.

"You're changing. I can feel it," Kich said and he looked down.

I had never saw Kich like this and it was breaking my heart.

I couldn't watch it and in my fucked up brain it translated as "do the extreme." I snatched my arm away from Kich.

"I can't fucking breath in this house. Just let me be," I said.

I turned my back quickly and I kept up the stairs. My heart was beating through my chest. I expected to feel Kich's hands grab me by my hair and pull me back down. But it never came. I don't know what Kich did because in my feeble attempt to prove a point I never turned around. He was right. I was changing. Was it Lamont? Or was it just me?

Was the girl who enjoyed all those crazy things starting to die? A part of me hoped not because I needed her.

Alter ego
I push you forward to deal with this shit.
The trauma, the rape, the situationships.
It's not fair to you but I can't handle our truth.
The reality is I'm not as strong as you.
If it hurts me too bad then off I go spiraling.
But you're built to last
I'm convinced you will die this way.
If I have to push through
just to get through the day...
You're the one who will come take my place.
Maybe I don't give you enough credit.
When it's said and done
you're the only one who gets it.
I use to look at you as the bad part of me
for participating and even enjoying all these
fucked up things.
But now I know
you're more of a hidden strength.
You're willing to fight for our destiny.
Arguably you're the best of me.

I turned over and picked up my phone. I didn't have anything from Kich but I had a message from Lamont.

Lamont

I miss you.

  I contemplated. I wiggled my lips, I bit them, I puckered them. I paced my eyes back and forth and then I did it.

           I miss you too.

  I knew it was wrong. But wrong was something I had gotten used to doing. What harm could one reply do?

Chapter 3

Love Of My Life

"So you think you're something because you've never used a safeword before," Melanie teased.

"I'm just not a punk ass bitch like you," I smiled.

"No, he just takes it easy on you," she said.

"Girl you use safe words even if you cum too much. Like seriously just let that shit flow," I said.

"I've never used a safeword with you," she said.

"And what does that mean? You know I be having you cumming back to back," I defended.

"Hmmmph," she stood up in her daisy dukes, no top, and perky breast just eyeing me. She turned and switched out of the room.

"Hey we aren't done here. You forgot to confirm I was telling the truth," I yelled.

Just then Kich was entering into the living room. I sat there with my foot thrown over the couch in a black one-piece spaghetti strap and shorts set. Kich came directly to me and started to massage my feet. I looked him deep in his eyes and he into mine. I loved that man but so much was different. He could feel it and I could too.

My difference was guilt. His difference was intuition. It's something about being all in someone's soul and knowing when they've changed. We were soultied and Kich could feel that my soul had begun to waver. I was confused. I had been getting more messages from Lamont and I didn't know what to do about it. I was getting older and with Lamont I had a chance at something normal. With Lamont I could build a traditional family and try to live happily ever after. With Kich we could never be normal. And the worst of it all was I didn't know what I wanted. I didn't know who I wanted to appease more.

Kich grabbed my hand and pulled me up. He then sat down in my spot that had been warmed by my pressing vagina heating up during Mel's and my sex talk. Kich pulled me onto his lap.

"Vistoria, relationships go through things. Communication and understanding is how we get through things," he said.

"I know Kich," I said.

"Well then tell me," he said.

"I'm ready. What's different? Is it anything I can help you with?" he asked.

I hated when Kich did this. I hated when he blamed himself for my shortcomings.

"Kich it's not you. It was never you," I paused.

Bitch are you really going to tell him?

I didn't want to be a liar anymore. But then I tried to speak and the words just wouldn't come out.

"Ok, so are you going to tell me what it is then?" Kich looked puzzled.

"It's just me. Internally. I need to work on myself that's why I've been spending so much time alone. I can't fully pour into someone's cup if my cup is empty," I stated.

"I couldn't agree more. Which is why I think you should get out today. Go wherever you want. Rico can drive you or not. I want you to start working on yourself. I like this," Kich said.

So upon Kich's request I went and got dressed in search for some me-time. Kich could be overbearing at times. Most times he had Rico drive us when he wasn't driving us because he was overprotective and a flat out stalker. I had started to get into astrology more and I couldn't wait to do Kich's chart. He and Mel didn't really get into it that much but I liked it. I knew Kich was a Libra and Mel a Cancer but I wanted to know more.

I bet Kich is a Scorpio Moon or maybe even a Taurus Moon. Nah he ain't traditional at all. Possessive yeah. But Taurus moon take a lifetime to commit that's not Kich. My money is back on Scorpio Moon.

Although Kich had a garage full of cars and some were brand spanking new I opted for the ole BMW i8 because it was still my favorite.

My first stop was the crystal store. I wanted to see if I connected with any new crystals. I also wanted a clear quartz pendulum and a deck of tarot cards. I figured it was no time like the present to start learning more and connecting with the things my soul had been resonating with.

I circled the block a few times when I arrived to the crystal store looking for a spot. There was one right by the door entrance but it was a parallel park. I bit my lip and contemplated if I felt like risking it with Kich's car. I decided to give it a go and to my surprise I had gotten a whole lot better at parking.

Parking just has never been my strong suit. Now that I had successfully parked I hopped out of the car and went in. As I opened the door there were chimes that went off greeting me. My inner witch smiled.

"Welcome, let me know if there is anything I can help you with," said the guy behind the counter. He had a rustic brown skin tone, with brown eyes, and silky twisted plats in his hair. He looked like he was around 5'9" and was average shape.

"Sure, I'm just happy to be here," I smiled.

And I was. It felt so peaceful and like everything I needed. I went to the crystal sections and brushed my fingers across the bins. There were big ones, small ones, chunky ones, and flat ones. There in the corner it caught my eye and my heart buzzed. I walked over to it and touched it. I felt a vibration. I picked it up and it shocked me. I felt the hairs on my arms stand up.

"Ahhh, Amethyst. I'm not surprised this one called out to you," he said.

"How much for this one?" I asked. I knew I had to have it. I had never felt a shock like that before.

"That one? $50 bucks," he said.

"Sold," I said. I went in my fanny pack and pulled out a hundred. I sat my other things on the counter and waited for my total.

"Keep the change," I smiled as I grabbed my bag.

"Thanks and please come again," he said as I was exiting.

"Oh I will," I said.

I felt good. This felt good. And at that moment I felt my phone vibrating and dinging.

I looked and it was Lamont. I hesitated. I knew I shouldn't answer. But I was a Sagittarius...we're always playing with fire.

Lamont

"Hello."

"What's up."

"Nothing much. I'm just wondering why you called me."

"Really Stori, why you gotta act like that? I'm just checking up on you and I wanted to hear your voice."

"Yeah, sure. Well I was just
about to go grab me
a bite to eat and head back home."

"Home, with your threesome family?"

"I don't need your judgment.
You already have an ex-wife before 30
remember?"

"Touche. Where are you
grabbing food from? Can I at least come to
meet you and pay for it?"

"You can pay for it
via cashapp if that's your goal.
So say what's really on your mind?"

"I want to see you."

"I'm probably just going to grab a bite to eat
from this side street store. You know how I am
when I'm in Memphis. I stan all the small
businesses."

"Well I'm there."

"Alright, well I'm gonna walk to it now. It's
like .5 miles up and I don't want to move my
car."

"I'll be there as fast as I can."

End call.

I sent Lamont my address as soon I hung up.

What the fuck are you doing?

I was so attached to my new things that I didn't bother putting them in the car. I walked with them and smiled the entire way. I made it to the restaurant pretty fast. About 15 minutes later Lamont was pulling up. And then it hit me....it hit me hard. I hadn't saw this man in years. I hadn't saw this man since he married another woman. I hadn't saw this man since he broke my fucking heart into pieces. I felt a panic attack happening. I wanted to scream. I wanted to cry. I wanted to fight.

I knew it was him by his head shape and he was driving the same car. Lamont was far from broke but frugal he was. This was the same car he had since early college. He parallel parked perfectly and got out. I saw him starting to walk over. I paced in my head what should be my first sentence.

Oh now you choose to be mute.

"You took long enough and now I want double the amount of food I was gone order cause I'm starving," I snapped.

In moments where my heart hurt the most I could always muster up a comment to make the other person seem small.

"That's fine. I will get you anything on the menu your stomach can hold. Although by the looks of it may not be a lot. You've lost a lot of weight," he said.

"Yeah you know. I've been working out and stressing cause the love of my life married someone else. It's easier than you know," I replied.

"I deserve that. Well hey, lets get that food shall we?" he reached for the door and I walked in.

This was one of those spots were we could just choose a seat. There was no greeter. We grabbed the 1st table that was empty and free of debris. There were already menus on the table.

"Do you know what you want?" Lamont asked.

"Yep, I want two extra long hot dogs with chili cheese tots," I said.

"Is that enough meat for ya," Lamont teased.

"Oh yes! I know I will only eat one now but the other is for later," I said.

"And what do you want to drink?" he asked.

"Water please," I said.

"All that junk and you got the nerve to order a water," he teased.

"Water is good for the hoo-ha," I laughed.

"Yeah...and your hoo-ha is yummy as fuck," he said.

Lamont ordered a hamburger and a sprite. We were pretty quiet while eating until he burst out in curiosity.

"So what's in the bag?" he asked.

"Just some stuff I got from the crystal store up the street," I said.

"Let me see," he reached for my bag.

"Tarot cards and giant rocks. Geesh what kinda things are you into now?" he asked.

"It's not a big deal. I like it. We are mystical creatures you know. Spiritual beings in a body. I'm just communing with my spirit," I said.

"Ok, well if you like it. Who am I to judge I barely pay attention in church as it is. I'm sure there are other spiritual ways out there. I've just never been much of an explorer," he said.

"Oh yeah, I know. Good and old fashioned is how you like it," I winced.

"Lamont, I'm on a path that is my own. Don't come in trying to change me. It will only make me run away faster," I said.

"I respect that. But I have another question. How are you on a path that's your own when you're in a poly relationship?" he asked.

"It's like building a house. A house isn't built with just one piece. All the pieces come together in their uniqueness and purpose for a finished product. It's the same. We are all individuals coming together to make a whole," I said.

"Did he teach you that response?" he asked.

"No, I just thought of it right here. I mean I am still a writer you know. That's my kind of thing. And can we lay off my man? You are my ex, remember?" I said.

"I'm your present and future but you just won't admit it," he smirked.

I rolled my eyes.

"Ok, so let's get on this book. What are you working on?" he asked.

"I have a children's book that I'm trying to get an agent to represent for me. So pray for me," I said.
"You sure you want me to pray for you? I don't believe we're talking to the same God anymore," he said.

"Oh wow...," I said and sipped my water. I drank it so fast I was now making slurping sounds.

"I don't think there's any left," he said.

I picked up my phone for the 1st time in this visit and started to read messages. Kich had text me like 5x.

Kich

Where are you?
Vistoria?
I haven't heard from you.
Are you ok?

This is why I don't
like you out alone.

And it kept happening.

Kich

I'm going to come
find you if I don't
get a response soon.

I knew I had to reply because I couldn't
be found doing this.

Kich

I'm ok. I got lost in
my head from so
much fun.

I was a horrible liar and Kich was
going to read through it.

"Is that him texting you back to back?"
Lamont asked.

"Yes," I said sharply.

"Someone has a God-complex," he
said.

"He doesn't. He's just concerned. He's protective and he cares about me," I defended.

"You're very defensive about him," he said.

"Do you know how long I defended you saying you weren't really with her. You didn't want her and then you go and marry the bitch. The one thing I got right was knowing y'all would divorce. You were always too good for her," I said.

He sat there with his mouth open.

"I gotta go. This was a mistake," I said as I gathered my food and my other things and headed for the door. I could see Lamont fidgeting to get his card and pay before I disappeared. I sped up even faster. I loved being dramatic. I got to my car so fast. Lamont was just now making it out of the restaurant. When he spotted me I was getting into the car and pulling the door down.

"Stori, Stori. Hey come on. I don't want it to end like this," he said as he was running up to my car.

I hit the gas and sped off.

"Fuck him. Love of my life? Yea fucking right. I was an idiot for coming and an idiot for ever loving you," I blasted some Meg and got my mind off him.

Chapter 4

Love Of My Now

"Is your breakfast not good?" Kich asked.

I was rolling my turkey sausage around in the plate and had taken one bite of my eggs.

"No, it's fine," I responded.

I was disgusted at myself but I couldn't stop. I knew I was pushing Kich away. I knew he was feeling unloved. I couldn't stop. I felt even more guilty. I felt even badder for leaving Lamont. I felt like a bad person all around. I couldn't figure out why anyone wanted to be with me.

Kich just looked at me. I was disappointing him and he didn't know how to fix me.

"I'm gonna go get some work done. I have some lyrics I need to write. Enjoy your breakfast ladies," Kich drank his juice and stood up.

Melanie took her knife and stabbed it in between my spread apart fingers.

"I will fuck you up," she said through her teeth.

"I'd like to see you try bitch," I said.

I knew I was wrong, but this bitch would never get the chance in her life to threaten me.

"You're destroying him. When I find out what you're up to I'm going to tell and I'm going to get you out of here. He deserves so much better than you," she said.

I normally have a bucket of clapbacks, but I was too tired to argue with Melanie.

I hopped up from the table.

"I'm done eating," I said.

I was headed up the stairs and I passed one of Kich's recording rooms. It sounded like he was writing a love song. I wanted to go in, but I didn't. I paused at the door and listened for a moment and then I kept walking. By the time I made it to the end of the hallway Kich was at the door.

"Did you need something?" he asked.

"Oh no, I didn't want to disturb you," I said. My eyes were fighting back tears at this point. I knew I loved Kich with every piece of my fiber. Lamont was the love of my life, but Kich was the love of my now and eternity. There's nothing he could ever do to make me love him less. And that's why I had to come clean.

"I...," I paused, it wouldn't come.

"Tell me," Kich pleaded at the door. This is what he had been waiting for.

"So the other day," I started but I couldn't finish.

"The other day....I purchased some tarot cards and I probably need more practice because I haven't pulled anything good," I said.

"Is that all you had to tell me?" he asked.

"Yes...I'm a little nervous. You know we're not supposed to play around with these things. I should give it a rest until I study more. I should also bond with my cards. That could be the issue," I said.

Kich looked relieved but not convinced.

"So we're having a small gathering tonight. Will you be my slave?" he asked.

I walked closer to him and put his finger down my throat.

"I'm a slaveeeeee...for you," I sang Britney Spears.

"I'll see you then. I'll text you what I'd like for you to wear. I'm gonna get this song finished," he said.

"Ok," and I turned to walk away.

He was still holding my hand. He pulled me back and grabbed my face. He squeezed my cheeks so tight until my mouth popped open a little. He spit in my mouth.

"Don't you ever forget who you belong to," he said.

I instantly got weak in the knees.

"Yes Sir," I said.

"Now you may leave," he said as he smacked my ass.

It's been a minute since we let loose and had one of our events. I was looking forward to it.

I went to my room and lied down. A few hours passed and I was getting photos from Kich of my attire. Kich wanted me in a complete fishnet outfit, masquerade mask, and barefoot .

I was happy it was simple, and I wouldn't have to be in heels all night. I took a bath and had all my smell goods. I found the fishnet look in my closet. I hadn't worn this one yet. I was just about to text Kich and ask him how to wear my hair when a message came in.

Kich

Natural hair.

My haircut had grown out and was already shoulder length. I put some keratin in it and did a light flat iron. I still wanted it to be bushy but just grabbable. I did my makeup. I did light foundation, highlighter, a red lip, and a cat eye. Cat eyes were Kich's favorite on me because he said I had eyes like a cat anyways.

It was time, so I walked to my door and waited for Kich. He arrived on time and added my leash to my outfit. Either Melanie didn't get invited to this event or she was already down there being Melanie.

Kich and I entered his hosting area and as always it was extravagant. Guests watched as I walked in with Kich. I was his property and I knew it. The naked waitresses were always my favorite, but today Kich wanted me in submissive mode so I couldn't do too much without permission. I had my head down, but I was peaking from my peripheral at everyone there.

"Stop," Kich said.

"Kneel," he said.

"Head up," he ordered.

"Take this mask off and let them see your face," he snatched my mask off and I was already oozing on the floor.

He slapped me.

"I know you're not cumming already. Little whore," he said.

"I'm sorry," I whispered.

"Speak up they can't hear you," he said.

"I'm sorry," I said louder.

"What should I do with a whore who cums before she's even been touched," Kich asked.

I could look around the room and tell all the men wanted me. They wished I was their slave, but Kich would never allow it. He loved rubbing me in their faces. They could only have me if I chose them and still Kich would have to approve of it.

"Fuck her," one guy said.

"Shove your cock in her throat until she vomits," another said.

Kich wasn't appalled at any of it. We've been there done that.

"Make her fuck my horse," another guy said.

Kich looked in his direction.

"Now that's an interesting game of choice," Kich looked intrigued.

He wouldn't dare. Right?

Kich has to know. I've done some fucked up things. I am a twisted person, but I draw the line at kids and animals. No fucking way.

Give me a tranny I'll fuck the shit out of her. I'll ride the fuck out of her dick while sucking her tits. That'd be the best sex ever I'm sure.

The thought made me cum more, but I had to remember my current dilemma.

"And where's your horse now?" Kich asked.

"The people want to be entertained right here and now," Kich demanded.

My heart grew more and more.

Is Kich going to make me do this. I won't. But if I don't will he be mad at me? A fucking horse?

"It's back home. I'll drop big bucks to have her come over and fuck him. I'll have the horse monitored while they get it on," he said.

Kich's eyes were gleaming with what looked like excitement. He grabbed a drink from a waitress walking by with them.

"Stand," Kich demanded.

"Walk with me over to this gentleman," Kich said.

I put my head down and began walking.

"Head up dear," he said.

We were now face to face with this man who wanted me to screw his horse.

"Drink," Kich said.

I drank.

"Spit it in his face," Kich said.

I knew where this was going.

I cocked back a good gargle and let the man have it.

Kich released my leash and punched the guy. The guy fell back and caught himself on a nearby table.

"Have this piece of horseshit escorted out of my premises and banned for life from my events," Kich said.

"And if I ever see you again I just may kill you if you ever disrespect my Princess with such mediocrity of a fucking fetish. You throw your fucking money at me. You think a price would ever make me sell her. That goes to any of you sons of bitches and bitches of bitches. Do not ever fucking confuse who she is," Kich slammed the glass down so hard it broke in his hands.

He was bleeding.

"Kich," I said.

Melanie ran over.

"It's fine. Let the festivities continue," Kich said.

"Go get the 1st aid kit," Melanie said to one of the waitresses.

"Now," she screamed.

"Calm down Melanie. I am fine. Tonight was exhilarating. Was it not?" he asked.

Melanie had the kit by now and wrapped Kich's hands up.

"It may need stitches. I'll have Dr. Earl do a night visit when you're done," Melanie said.

She glared at me.

"The cut is small Melanie. See it's not even penetrating your bandages. I'll be fine. Go have a drink for me will you dear," he said.

"Yes Sir," she closed the kit and disappeared into the crowd.

"Now see...you have to do all the work. I still want to be fucked," Kich laid down on the open floor.

"Get busy and fuck me," he said.

I ripped open the vagina area of my fishnets and unbuttoned his pants. His dick was bulging, and I couldn't wait to feel the head going inside me.

I could feel eyes on my back and I was even more exuberant. Kich had made it known how much he cared for me in front of this entire party. There is nothing that could ever make me leave him. And I hoped there was nothing that would ever make him leave me.

Chapter 5

End of my Love

The night ended and I can't truly recall what all happened. I just know I woke up with all my holes still oozing. I remember taking shrooms, a pill, and even an edible. Who knows what the fuck I did! Kich was up and walking around. There were still guest asleep and some still fucking. When Kich noticed I was up he came over and lifted me.

"You were an awesome performer last night. You never take the drugs at my parties like you did last night. I don't know what got in you but I enjoyed it. I wouldn't make it a habit but this was nice," he said.

I smiled.

"Let's get you up to your room and nourished. I've already had them set up IV therapy in there. You're the only thing missing," Kich said.

Kich helped me up to my room and I got my therapy. He later had food brought to me as well. I was in bed asleep most of the day. I didn't even notice I hadn't seen my phone since last night. I feel like it was the next day before I was back to myself.

I walked downstairs and saw Kich in the kitchen reading and drinking tea.

"Good morning," I said.

"Well I think it's morning," I stated.

"It surely is. You slept for two days almost," he said.

"Have you seen my phone?" I asked.

"Yes it's over on the charging dock," he said.

"Did I get any messages?" I asked.

I had blocked Lamont so I knew there wouldn't be any from him.

"Honestly I didn't check," he said and walked over to pick it up.

My heart was racing although I knew he was blocked. Kich hadn't asked to go through my phone in forever, so I didn't think he was going to start.

He picked it up and looked down.

"Now that's interesting," he said.

My heart was pulsing through my shirt.

"What is?" I asked.

"An unsaved messenger asking when they can see you again," he said.

"Huh," I played dumb.

"Let me see," I said.

Kich had read my phone from the locked screen. I had meant to turn that off. But since I blocked Lamont I didn't think I needed to. I had no other skeletons kept from Kich.

I opened the phone and I immediately knew it was Lamont.

I text back.

(998)737-3822

When will I see
you again?

Who is this?

Your nail girl.
New number.

"Babe, it's just my nail tech. She has a new number," I said relieved.

She's probably wanting to make that extra money because I always give her great tips.

Kich was still glaring at me.

"Do you want to see the message?" I asked.

"Vistoria... I'm sure this is true but why are you pale as if you saw a ghost?" Kich asked.

"I'm only going to ask you this once," he said.

"And please do not lie because I hate a liar more than a cheater," he said.

"A cheater is a liar," I said with guilt.

I knew at this point I couldn't lie because Kich could've already had someone to spy on me.

"I was feeling lost a few weeks ago. Things felt different with us. I started to doubt what I wanted and where we stood," I started.

Kich was now gripping the table firmly and I grew more afraid.

"What did you do?" he asked.

"I had lunch. That's all," I said.

"With whom?" he asked.

"Lamont," I said.

"Your ex?" he asked.

"Your 1st love?" he continued.

"Don't say it like that. There's nothing between us and I was just going there to test it out. I realized there's no one I love more than you," I said but Kich interrupted.

"Vistoria save it. I have tried and all you do is lie and use me. You're selfish and ungrateful. I can't continue this. I can't keep giving you all of me and you're not reciprocating. This is the end of my love. It has run out for you," Kich said.

"What? Well that can't be," I said.

"I didn't sleep with him or anything," I defended.

"You're being so close minded. I have been in a relationship with myself longer than I have been in a relationship with you. But when I got in a relationship with you it's like you wanted me to throw all that away. I started doing so much as a group with you and Mel. Then everything became a duplex or a threesome and nothing was just me anymore. So yes I started to seek my own company, yes my ex joined me one day, and YES he paid for my dinner one of those days. It was just a fucking hot dog and fries you make it sound so romantic. I'm lost. I'm losing myself and all you can think about is your fucking self," I pleaded.

"You're such a condescending, lying whore," Kich stormed out of the kitchen.

"Kich can we just talk about this?" I grimaced and looked away.

"Do you think this is a game? You've been in my house, spending my money, while secretly bonding with your ex. Do you remember why he's your ex?" Kich grabbed my arm.

"Ouch you're hurting me," I said.

He pulled me closer.

"You seem to think I care," he pushed me into the couch.

"What's wrong Kich? You can't take a little competition? You can't take a dose of your own medicine? What? You're the only person who can have multiple lovers?" I yelled.

"It's not the same and you know it," Kich gritted his teeth and I saw his jaw popping.

"Oh what's not the same about it?" I stood up tall and started walking towards him.

"Vistoria that's enough," Melanie said and grabbed my hand to pull me out of the room.

I snatched away.

"Oh no, I'm not done," I continued.

"Vistoria I said that is enough," Melanie repeated.

"Kich you can't take loving someone and knowing that person has a heart for someone other than you can it?" I got in his face.

"Vistoria you are out of line," Melanie pulled me back.

"Bitch get your hands off me," I screamed.

Kich continued looking down at the floor and his breathing became heavier.

"Get out Vistoria," Kich firmly stated.

"I'm not going anywhere," I said.

I could tell I was pissing Kich off but it was like I couldn't stop. I was all-in and I wanted to push him over the edge. I didn't know what was on the other side of the cliff, but I wanted to see it. I wanted to see just how far Kich could be pushed.

"I don't know what you hate more. The thought of me loving him or the thought of him fucking me," I said.

"So you still love him?" Kich stood up and glared at me.

Oh shit, I don't want to answer this question right now. I probably shouldn't have angled my argument here.

"Well no. I was confused before I saw him but now I know," I started and Kich cut me off.

"You're such a fucking liar. You aren't going behind my back with this nigga if it wasn't love. Is your life worth risking for a nigga you don't love?" Kich asked.

"Are you threatening me? Fuck this. You don't have to put me out. I'll leave. I'm so tired of this unstable relationship. All you know is control. You don't know love," I said.

"I don't know love? What have I controlled? You do whatever you want while spending my money. All I ever asked was for you to be honest with me. You're a manipulative, little bitch. You can't admit that you wanted to keep me just how I was while building this relationship with your past love. You didn't tell me he took you to dinner because you knew that I would know it meant more to you and him. Get out," he said.

"You don't know me," I turned and began exiting the room.

"And I'm not leaving until I pack my things up. I don't know who you think you are," I yelled as I headed up the stairs to my room.

Kich stumbled towards his Steinway in the middle of the room. He sat at his chair. There was a vase full of roses on top, and I wondered if he would throw them at me.

I continued to throw my things around the room as I packed.

"And don't take anything I bought you," I could hear Kich yelling from downstairs.

"Can you pull up to the front of the house and get my bags," I called Rico on his cell.

"Yes Ms. Jefferson, I'm pulling up now," he said.

I began carrying bags downstairs and setting them by the door so Rico could pack them in the suburban.

I galloped back up the stairs and continued packing different items Kich had bought. I knew he was only speaking from anger. He didn't care about any of that stuff. I carried another bag downstairs.

I could hear Melanie comforting him from the other room.

I continued to pack my Louis Vuitton duffels and place them by the door.

"I thought I said not to take anything I bought. I'm pretty sure my money bought those last two duffels," Kich said from the living room.

"You bought it for me so it's mine," I said.

Kich stood up and he knocked the vase of roses onto the floor.

I turned around and saw him coming closer to me.

"Oh what you're going to hit me now," I said as I turned to head back up the stairs.

"Purple," Kich said as he came closer to me.

Melanie jumped in front of him.

"Kich no purple. No purple. I'll handle it. Please just give me a chance to handle it," she said. She was trying to plant her feet on the ground and stop him, but he was practically scooting her with him.

"Purple…what does purple mean?" I said.

"Vistoria, you need to go. It's not safe for you to be here anymore," she said.

Purple....is that a code? I can't remember what it meant. But I think it means something bad because Kich looks furious.

And then I was unable to stop.

"Kich what the fuck does purple mean? Huh?" I said.

"You'd know if you actually paid attention to any of the rules he gives us. But it's obvious that I'm the only one who does," Melanie said.

"Yeah cause you're Kich's little ro-bitch," I joked.

"You know. I was kinda starting to like you. I mean really like you not what I had been pretending to do since I met you. And now you pull this and to make matters worse you seem as if you don't care," Melanie admitted.

Oh right. Purple was a safe word for if I'm being choked too tightly. Basically it means I can't breath. I guess Kich is warning that he's gonna choke me.

"Get the fuck out," Kich yelled. He was trying harder and harder to get to me and it was that moment I felt I had went too far.

I started to back up to the door and I turned the knob. Kich lunged at me and I snatched it open and pulled it up from the other side, but I could feel his strength subduing me.

"Kich please," Melanie was trying to calm him from the other side. I felt the door loosen. I took that moment to run to the truck parked in front of the house.

"Rico, go. It's Kich. He's going to hurt me," I said frantically.

"Ms. Jefferson I'm sure that's not what's happening. I'm sure it's all a misunderstanding," Rico said.

"He said purple. I could be dumb, but I'm sure that was a warning using one of our safe words," I said.

"Oh shit. I better get you out of here Ms. Jefferson," Rico started the truck.

As soon as he started it I looked up to the door and Kich was coming out.

"Rico, don't leave," he said.

"Rico....leave," I said.

"Mr. Montel you'll thank me later," Rico said.

Kich was reaching for the door just as Rico was pulling off.

"If she wants to leave me that bitch can call a fucking Uber," Kich yelled as we were leaving.

I turned around and looked out of the tinted windows and saw Kich's entire body go limp as he caved to the ground.

Is he crying?

Melanie rushed to his side and cradled next to him. I saw her glaring at the truck. I stared back in regret as they began to disappear in the sandstorm the tires had created.

Chapter 6
<u>Single Again</u>

Being back at my mom's house was the most ghetto shit I could've ever done. I felt disgusted with myself every day I woke up under her prissy ass roof and being everything I wasn't. She wanted me to go to church on Sundays. I hadn't seen a church in years. The more I refused the more she thought I was a witch or a devil worshiper.

"So you went to college to become this?" my mom asked as she walked in the room and opened my blinds.

"I went to college to learn skills that would prepare me to be my own boss," I said.

"You could've watched YouTube for that and saved me and your father $50,000," she said.

"Would you like me to have Kich pay you back?" I asked.

"That's not the point Vistoria," she said.

"I'm sure you paid more of that $50,000 than Dad did," I said.

"Your father helped. Don't be that way," I said.

"And if we're really keeping it a hundred...Papa's life insurance had a sum in there for me. So let's not act like you and Daddy are saints," I said.

"I don't know where you get that mouth from, but you will not speak to me in that manner in my house. You can go live with your father," she said.

"Why would I want to go live with that drunk?" I asked.

"I'm gonna look over all of this mindless chatter since I know you're having a hard time," she said.

"Sure Pene. That's probably best," I said.

"I'd offer you breakfast but all you seem to consume these days are those tasteless green smoothies," she said.

"Thanks Mom," I said sarcastically.

My mom wasn't doing anything wrong, but I wasn't in the mood. I could hear the truth in my head circulating every day and I didn't need it from her.

She also didn't know I was bluffing about Kich. He hadn't spoken to me or returned any calls I made. My messages weren't delivering. I was either blocked, he broke that phone, or threw it in the Mississippi River. It didn't stop me from trying. I knew I could just drive to his house but I kinda wanted an ok. I didn't have the balls to pop up on Kich. It's crazy how a breakup could make me doubt everything we ever were. I guess because I also knew that love and hate may fall on two ends of the spectrum but they meet. They mate, they blend, and when a person does what I did to Kich, they marry.

Days passed and my heart ate at my chest. This felt like a death. I felt like I was losing Papa all over again. This felt worse than when me and Lamont split. Days passed, months passed...the sickness in my stomach grew worst. And then it eventually grew numb.

Black Hole
I loved you on purpose.
Oh what a waste that was.
I hate wasted time.
I'd rather waste my wine.
You'd rather waste a dime.
Well go get in line.
In line with all the ones
I thought you were different than.
See I thought you were a different man.
It turns out you're an imitation,
just like them.
You had no vision.
If you had vision
you would know that you were
winning.
All the times I could've left,
but I stayed.
See this is the shit
that makes me feel played.
I wasn't perfect,
but I know I was worth it.
I just needed you to wait on me.
I just needed you to have faith in me.
Now my heart has no trust
because when I needed you most
you lost faith in us.

Chapter 7

New Beginnings

Fall was my favorite time to be outdoors. I was starting to get pimples from not getting enough fresh air. My mom was worried beyond measures. I had mourned Kich's and my relationship long enough. He had not come back for me yet, and I knew it was time to move on.

I woke up that crisp morning in October and decided I wanted to take a run. I had placed my phone in the closet on airplane mode so this was the 1st time I had saw it in weeks. I pulled it down and found my airpods. I placed my phone on the charger so it could get a little juice.

I put on some leggings, sneakers, and a cute shirt. I had lost so much weight from stressing, but my boobs didn't go anywhere. I was happy about my waistline.

I should stress out more often.

I put my hair up in a high bun. My mom was shocked to see me out my room and dressed.

"Well, this is new or maybe it's old," she said.

"What mom?" I smiled a little.

"This is just refreshing. I'm happy to see you doing better. It's been months," she said.

I swallowed hard.

"Well I won't mention that. Enjoy your day sweetie," she said as she kissed me.

My mom headed to work and I darted out the door for my run.

The air felt amazing on my skin. I started running so fast that I forgot to turn my phone on and play music. Nature sounded amazing to me. I ran so far and so fast that by the time I felt my knees aching I was miles from home.

Fuck now I gotta go back.

Fuck that.

I was now feeling faint. I decided to call an Uber or Lyft because I wasn't running back home. My adrenaline had run out and reality had kicked in. My phone was still low so I needed this driver to get there quickly.

I decided to use Uber since I could get points for it. My driver was 3 minutes away.

I needed him to hurry because I was getting messages from everyone. From what I could see none of them were Kich.

I pushed the thought to the back of my mind because none of it mattered.

My ride pulled up.

"Brett?" I said.

"Kich?" he said.

My eyes instantly watered.

"What?" I said.

"Why'd you say that name? How do you know Kich?" I asked.

He was now looking a bit nervous but he responded.

"Your profile is under the name Kich and it even has a dude's picture up there," he said.

I had totally forgot that Kich replaced my profile with one he set up so men would think they were picking up a guy.

"I totally forgot. My boy.... sorry. My ex set it up that way. Looks like I need to change it. I haven't taken an Uber or used my phone since our breakup," I said.

"Well we can finish talking about this while I drop you off. If you wanna get in the car," he said.

"Yeah, sure. I'm holding you up. You have plenty of other people to pick up," I said as I got in the backseat.

"So do you wanna talk more about this breakup?" Brett asked.

I looked up into his blueish, green eyes. I hadn't realized how handsome he was 'til now.

He had a clean smile, brown hair, nice body, and I liked how he dressed.

"No, I don't," I said.

"Well you wanna talk about our 1st date?" he asked.

"Our....ha. Oh, so you're slick," I said.

"I like what I see so I'm gonna go for it," he said.

"I wasn't expecting this. I don't know if I'm even ready for a date to be honest," I said.

"I have time. Just leave me with your number or IG so you can reach out to me when you are ready," he said.

"I can do that," I said.

I ended up getting his number and giving him mine and my social profiles.

"Thanks for the ride...definitely 5 stars," I said as I was getting out.

That was the 1st time I had smiled in forever. It still hurt to smile. Every time I smiled I felt the tears in the corners of my eyes ready to release. I would breath deeply to move them around.

I walked back in the house and it was quiet. My mom hadn't made it back yet. I decided to reply to some of the messages I had received. Kara was in there. I hadn't talked to her in so long.

Kara

Stori please?

I'm here at mom's. Come over.

Lamont was in there.

Lamont

I love you and
I hope you're ok.

I need to see
you.

No Kich. No Melanie. Not even Rico. It was like that part of my life had just ended. The thought made me sick to my stomach.

And before I knew it I was crying again. I couldn't live without him. I didn't want to. I made my way to my mom's medicine cabinet and I took whatever I saw. I didn't care what it was. I didn't want to be here. God or whoever in charge could do me favor and release me. I wanted a new beginning, in a new planet, with some new creatures.

Get me the fuck out of here.

I could feel the 1st set of pills kicking in. So I did the last crazy thing.

Kich

I love you so
much that it's
probably illegal.
It's probably insane.
It's the end of me.
I cannot do this.
I cannot live
without you.
If I have to live
without you then
I won't live at all.

I knew it wouldn't deliver, but I
watched. And right before I passed out ...it
delivered.

Chapter 8

<u>Death</u>

"I love her. I need to fucking see her. This is my fault," Kich said.

"Kich," I said faintly.

"Get the hell out," my mom yelled.

"He is not welcome here. I am filing a restraining order as soon as possible," my mom continued.

"You can't keep me away from her," he said.

"Oh as long as she's at my house...yes I can," she said.

"I better not see you no where near our house," she said.

"You're not helping. You're making her worst. She did this because she thinks I'll never speak to her again," Kich said.

"I need her to know I love her and I'd never leave her," Kich said.

"You're the devil. You're the reason my daughter is messed up now. I hate you. Stay away from my family," she said.

"Kich....just go. I'll let you know when she wakes up," Kara said.

"No you won't," my mom said to Kara.

"Kich go," Kara said softly.

All of this felt like a dream. I thought I had created it all until Kara confirmed it. I fought to get back to Kich. His voice gave me the strength I needed.

I know you think this isn't love. But don't blame Kich. I'm the one who wanted to die. Kich didn't tell me to do that.

I opened my eyes.

"Kich," I whispered.

"I'm here," Lamont said.

"Hi," I said.

"Hey beautiful," he said.

"I'm glad you came. I did something stupid," I said.

"No...no...you're not stupid," he reassured.

I started to cry.

"What's wrong with me?" I asked.

"We're going to get you help," he said.

"Stori!" Kara ran over.

"Pene, she's up," Kara went to get my mom.

I was expecting judging eyes from my mom. I felt embarrassed. Instead she walked up and held me really close and started crying.

"Mom I'm ok," I said.

"I'm ok mom," I repeated.

"Mom....it's ok," I said.

"Hey.....stop crying," I said as tears formed.

"I'm here," I said.

She pulled back and looked at me.

"Stori...why didn't you tell me? You should've told me. I'm so sorry. I missed all the signs. You seemed ok this morning. I thought you were better. It was the 1st day I didn't stress. I felt we had hit a breakthrough. I just knew my prayers had been answered," she cried.

"Mom, I'm sorry," I cried.

The nurse came in.

"Ms. Jefferson when you're ready we have some questions to ask you and we'd like to set up your treatment going forward," she said.

"Treatment," I said.

"Yes, I figured we'd get you set up on anti-depressants and a psychiatrist," my mom chimed in.

"I'm not that bad mom. I don't need all of that," I said.

"Vistoria you scared me to death. You almost died. I don't want to hear that you don't want to do this," she said.

"You can't make me," I said.

"I can have you locked up. Because as of right now I am still responsible for you. Especially in this state. You're not in your right mind. So if you don't want to be locked away. I'd listen up," she said.

I couldn't blame her, but I was furious.

"I wanna be alone," I said.

"I'm sorry, but right now we can't leave you alone," the nurse said.

"Ok, I want to be alone with my best friend," I said.

"I'll stay. I'll make sure she's good," Kara said.

"I am not your enemy Vistoria," my mom said as she walked out.

Lamont kissed my forehead.

"I'll wait out here for you until you're ready. I'm not leaving your side," he said.

I couldn't wait for it to be Kara and me.

"Am I crazy? Did I hear Kich?" I asked.

"Don't answer that 1st question," I said.

"Yes. I mean yes you heard him," she said.

"How is he?" I asked.

"He was torn apart seeing you like this. They made him leave. They banned him from seeing you. Your mom says she's pressing charges," Kara said.

"Like hell she is. She can't do that. I need him," I said.

"Stori...I think it's over. This is it. Your mom isn't going to allow you to be with him. And who knows how long you have to show good behavior to get your rights back," Kara said.

"They can't take my rights," I said breathing deeply.

"I didn't harm anybody," I said.

"I think the rule is you can't be a harm to someone else or yourself," she said.

"I need to see him," I said.

"Where's my phone?" I asked.

"Your mom trashed it," Kara said.

The night ended and before I knew it I was in psych sessions listening to some bitch tell me I had daddy issues. I didn't need my mom to pay to have someone tell me that. But my daddy issues weren't why I loved Kich. I loved Kich because he completed my heart. Kich was the part I always needed. Kich was me.

"Vistoria, do you feel like talking today?" the psychiatrist asked.

I sat there staring into space.

"I'd love to give a good report and say you're getting better, but I have no idea because you don't talk to me," she said.

Now the bitch is blackmailing me. Isn't this illegal?

This shit was the most annoying part of my life, but I started cooperating and got better. I flushed the pills. I never believed in those shits.

Chapter 9

Life

While I was surviving life without Kich I did the one thing I was to used to.

F U C K.

The candidate this time was Brett. I would sneak out like it was high school because I didn't want my mom to know. I honestly didn't want anyone to know. Brett was nothing more than a rebound and he had poison. He was like every other toxic person in my life and toxic part of me. He was dark. It was different, but it was a fix.

"I'm so in love with your black pussy," he said.

"Shut up," I said as I grinded him hard in the front seat of his Camaro.

"Your pussy is so soft and hot," Brett continued.

"Uh huh," I said.

I just wanted him to shut the fuck up so I could cum and move on.

The one thing I liked about Brett was he had stamina. He could last so long. Sometimes I would cum multiple times before he was finished.

"Can I take you back to my place tonight?" Brett asked.

"I know you can go all night, but I really need to be getting back inside," I said.

"You're no fun," he teased.

"Tomorrow I'm gonna go spend some time with my cousin Cookie, so I'll stay with you after," I said.

"So why can't you just stay with me to stay with me?" he asked.

"You don't think I notice that you don't want anyone to know about me? Is it cause I'm just a rebound or is it cause I'm white?" he asked.

If he only knew I've slept with men and women of every race. It's definitely part of the 1st question and that my mom is on my ass about getting back with Lamont. Lamont is the only guy I've ever brought home that mom liked. Mom only liked Lamont so much because he got Papa's approval before he died. She feels like that means we are meant to be. But if God chose Lamont and Satan chose Kich then I sold my soul.

"I was always told you shouldn't ask questions that you don't want the answer to," I said as I slid my underwear on.

"I want the answer no matter what it is. I'm really into you and I just wanna know where I stand in your head. I figured when we 1st started talking I was a rebound but all this time and nothing has changed? You won't let me take you out. I can't come in your house and meet anyone. You talk about your best friend but I've never saw her either," he ranted on.

"I just need to feel something. I am dead inside. Kich has my soul no one fucking understands that. I will never be the same. I will never love the same. What we shared wasn't just love it was dominion," I said.

"How do you know I can't be that for you?" he asked.

"You can't and that's ok. I'm not with you so you can be him. I'm with you so you can be you. I enjoy my time with you. That's enough," I said.

The Sagittarius in me was jumping out. I was maneuvering this conversation like I was a guy. I got fully dressed and I sat in his car for a few more minutes. He kept trying to kiss on me and get back in my pants.

"I said we would see each other again tomorrow. I'm heading back in. Goodnight," I said.

I got out his car and headed back in the house.

He could never be Kich. There are three things Kich would've asserted with me. 1. Kich would've told me we were together. 2. Kich would've fucked me until I was ragged. 3. Kich wouldn't have let me leave if he wasn't ready to release me.

The thought of him or anyone trying to replace Kich made me sick. I knew I couldn't afford to spiral again, so I turned on some white noise, got my weighted blanket, and went to sleep.

I woke up the next morning to my mom with a tray in her hand and her placing it on my dresser.

"Wake up sleepy head. I made you breakfast," she said.

She didn't know I had just got back in the house a few hours before this, so I was extremely exhausted. I didn't want her to feel like her efforts were wasted, so I amped myself up. I somehow sat up in the bed and pulled the tray in my lap.

"So how are you feeling? You're looking so much better these days. You've gained some weight back. Well you know...healthy looking weight. It looks really good. I haven't seen you this full in a really long time," she said.

"Thanks Mom," I said as I bit into my french toast.

"It's good seeing you back happy and eating," she said.

I forced a smile.

"What are your plans today?" she asked.

"I'm probably going to go hang with Cookie and my friend Brett," I said.

"You and Cookie...y'all are like night and day Stori," she said.

"Mom...what do you mean?" I drank some of my milk.

"Cookie is so wild and she's always with men. Those men always buying her stuff and let's just say I'm glad you're nothing like her," she continued.

"Mom...I'm worst," I said.

"I highly doubt that," she said.

"Ignorance is bliss," I mumbled.

"What'd you say?" she asked.

"Oh nothing," I said.

"Have you talked to Lamont lately?" she asked.

I started to cram my food in my mouth because I was getting over the 3rd degree from my mom.

Am I allowed to plead the 5th to my parent?

"Umm, yeah the other day," I said.

"I like him," she continued.

"I know Mom," I said.

"Y'all would be so good together," she said.

"Well I'll be hanging with my friend Brett tonight. He's pretty cool too," I said.

"Well I'm sure he's no Lamont dear," she said.

"Nope, he didn't run off and marry another bitch on me," I said as I grabbed my tray and headed to the kitchen.

"Vistoria, that is no way to talk to me. You get back here and apologize," she demanded.

"Mom, maybe you're the one who should apologize to me. You assume things about my life and my friends yet you don't know me. You constantly put me off on Lamont because he's my only ex who makes you comfortable. I could live a normal southern life with him. But you forget the heartbreak he caused me. Everyone forgets the heartbreak he caused me. Every single thing he's doing now it's owed to me. He fucking owes me for what he did to me. I loved him and he lied to me. He looked me in my eyes and lied to me. I was in college trying to better myself. I thought he of all people would respect that. Instead what did he do? He goes and marries the woman who he told me it was nothing. The woman he told me not to worry about. So excuse me if I don't give a fuck...'excuse my language' of what anyone wants between us," I said.

"OK I'll leave it alone," she said and passed me to head to the living room.

"Mom I'm sorry," I said.

"It's ok. As a mom I just want the best for you," she said.

"No, I've never talked to you like I have been lately and it's not acceptable. I'm going to do better. You have always wanted the best for me and I know that. You're the only person who has my back no matter what and I can't take that for granted," I hugged her.

Maybe I should date more if Lamont is the best I have to offer.

I showered and got dressed. I hit Brett to come drop me off at Cookie's. She was at one of her dude's house, but it might as well have been hers. Cookie ran all her men.

We pulled up to her crib.

"So I guess I'll see you later?" Brett asked.

"You can come in and hang for a bit if you want," I said.

I realized whether Brett was a rebound or not I could at least treat him like a human. I didn't have to keep excluding him and keeping him in the dark.

"Sure. Yea," he said trying to hide his excitement.

Brett parked the car outside one of the 6 car garage doors. And then we heard Cookie on a speaker somewhere.

"I'm opening the door you can just park it in the last entrance," she said.

The door began to open and Brett drove in.

"Now how do we get in the house?" I said aloud.

There weren't any doors in this part.

I called Cookie and her voice came on the speaker again.

"There's a door that leads to the middle garage and there's an elevator there," she said.

We looked and looked, but I didn't see a door.

"Cook I don't see a door," I said.

Next thing I know the wall was opening and Cookie was standing before me.

"I mean I know it's hidden but use your imagination bitch," Cookie teased as she reached to hug me.

We laughed.

"Bitch what kind of futuristic shit is this?" I laughed.

"Girl we are in 2020. This is how the fuck we should be living," she said.

We finally got in the elevator after going through this Scooby-Doo ass house.

"You have a very lovely home," Brett said.

"Thanks boo. He's cute Stori," she said.

"Ok well I got shit to do. We'll kick it later, but make yourselves at home. Just don't get lost cause that's gonna fuck up my day," she said.

"Cookie what all is in this house?" I asked.

"Girl everything. Enjoy," she said.

Brett and I stayed together and close. We gave ourselves a house tour.

There really was everything in there. There was a hibachi area, a nail salon, a movie theater, and we found it. The sex room. There was literally porn playing in it when we walked in. Glory holes and more were waiting to be explored.

If I didn't know better I'd say this was Kich's doing.

"Let's try the glory hole," Brett said.

I had no idea if a room like this had cameras, but I'm sure I've been caught doing worse.

Brett went into the entrance of the glory hole and he had his dick sticking out in no time.

Brett had a nice size dick. I was a little surprised, but I was also grateful. Penis was like a Cracker Jack box... I never knew what I was gonna get.

I pulled off my pants and got positioned.

We probably should be using a condom.

The thought crossed my mind, but I was already arching my back and sliding Brett inside. He had never came in me, so I didn't think I had anything to worry about.

This glory hole also had arm holes so Brett was sticking his arms through and spanking me. He would pull my waist and hold me closer.

"I'm so fucking in love with you," he said.

That's not creepy at all Brett. You love me and all we do is fuck.

I got turned around and got on my knees to suck his dick through the hole.

I was deepthroating and slobbing all over it.

"Get back on it," Brett said.

We had fun in that room. Brett came faster than normal, but I suppose it was the new environment exciting him.

After we finished we laid out in the floor. Brett made me feel something. It wasn't love but it was a bit of life.

Chapter 10

Retrograde

A few weeks after that date I was laid up at my mom's house and feeling horrible.

I had been throwing up all morning, and every thing in the house made me sick.

Lamont had been hitting me up faithfully asking to take me out on a date. I just wasn't interested. There would have to be some catastrophic event that would make me take Lamont seriously. We just weren't the same anymore. He reads a Bible for directions and I consult the spirits and read cards.

The next few days I was in pain. My abdomen area was hurting and my boobs were super tender. I wasn't really on my period, but I was seeing some blood here and there. I figured I was just having a bad case of PMS. This had happened to me once in college, and I was also vomiting.

"Stori, you've been under the weather a while now. You may need to go to the doctor. I've added you back on my insurance, so it should be no issue," my mom said.

"Ok," I said and rolled over in the bed.

"Do you have a way there?" she asked.

"Yes, my friend Brett can take me," I said.

"Alright, well let me know how it goes," she said.

I mustered up some hand strength to text Brett.

Brett

> Hey can you pick me up? I need to go to the doctor. I haven't gotten better.

Yea. Time?

> Let me see if they can take a walk-in.

I set my appointment for the next 2 hours because they had availability. I let Brett come in with me because I needed the support. My abdomen area was hurting so bad I could barely walk.

"Well Ms. Jefferson I'm surprised you made it here with what you're suffering from," the doctor said.

A sense of worry crossed my face.

"We want to look further and do an ultrasound on you, but you're definitely positive. Add that with your symptoms it seems you're having an ectopic pregnancy," she said.

"A what?" I asked as my eyes began to water.

"Pregnancy," I said in between gasps.

Brett squeezed my hand.

"How can I save my baby?" I asked.

It was like a maternal instinct kicked in.

"Well...Ms. Jefferson the thing about these pregnancies are the chances of saving the baby is rare. Your baby is possibly growing in the fallopian tube or somewhere else causing you harm. It is better for the mom to terminate the pregnancy," she said.

"Wow...I just found out I'm pregnant and here you are telling me there's no chance to save my baby," I said.

"Well that's why we want to do the ultrasound to see," she continued.

"No, nooo, you will not get another dime from me just to tell me my baby won't make it," I said.

"I will die if it means my baby could live," I said.

"I'm ready to go Brett," I turned to him.

He lifted me up instantly.

"Ms. Jefferson what you're doing is fatal to yourself," she said.

"Can you make me stay?" I asked.

"No," she said.

"Well then I'm leaving," I said.

It was a long car ride back home in silence.

"I know someone who had this happen. The baby had to be removed Stori," Brett said.

"I don't want to talk about this," I said.

We pulled up to my mom's house and Brett helped me inside.

My mom wasn't there yet.

"Thank you for all your help, but I'd like to be alone," I said.

"Stori, I'm worried. That's our baby inside of you, but I want to know you both are ok. If this one doesn't work out we can always try again," he said.

The thought of him already planning the death of our baby disgusted me.

"I want to be alone," I said.

Brett left.

I sat in my room crying for hours. I crawled to the bathroom because the pain was getting unbearable.

I sat on the toilet and I talked to my unborn.

"Hey, you there. Why now are you choosing me? I'm a fuck up. I don't have shit to my name right now. I'm surviving off my mom. I sold my car and let a guy give me a car only for him to take it back when we broke up so now I'm carless. I don't have a job either, but if you come I'll promise I'll take care of you. But.....," my tears increased at my next sentence.

"But if you could just give mommy a chance to get some things right 1st I will love you even harder and better. I guess what I'm asking is can you just wait? Mommy won't abort you. Mommy won't get you surgically removed, but if you can just do this for mommy our life will be better. If you could just wait a little longer. I thank you for showing mommy exactly what she was missing. I thank you for showing mommy it's time for her to grow up, but just give mommy a chance to make things right. It's your choice, but I will die having you if you want to come. I will make that sacrifice," I said.

A day passed. Bleeding continued. I cleaned up after myself like things were normal. I was in excruciating pain.

"Hush little baby don't say a word. Mommy's gonna buy you a mocking bird. And if that mocking bird don't sing. Mommy's gonna buy you a diamond ring," I sang as I applied to jobs.

My credit was still good so I applied for a car online. It wasn't fancy but it was a car I could pay off fast. I knew I didn't want any debt with a new baby coming.

Brett

How are things?

I'm great. I just got approved for a new car I just gotta go check it out and things. I'm trying to wait until I feel a little better.

Stori it's probably
time to get that
ultrasound and just
be sure of what's
going on.

It's common for
women to bleed
during pregnancies.
How can they
diagnose me for
ecotopic without
doing an ultrasound?

Another day passed. I was still in pain
and bleeding. The bleeding was getting
chunkier but I stayed the course. My baby and
I were in this for the long haul. I got my old
job back editing and thank God it was done
from home. As I was editing I ignored a lot of
the pain I was in.

Another day and I didn't see any blood
and I was in less pain.

See we're making this work.

Another day...no blood and no pain.

I wanted to go to the doctor to show
them I had overcome. I hadn't found the time
to pick up my car yet, so I text Brett.

Brett

> Hey. The bleeding
> stopped. I'm ready
> to go to the doctor.
> I already set an
> appointment it's at 10.

We got to the doctor and the 1st thing
they did was test me again. I was still positive.
I smiled.

"Let's do this ultrasound," I said.

The doctor began setting me up. I laid
down on the table, and she rubbed the cold gel
on my stomach.

"I want to apologize for assuming what
you were going through was an ectopic
pregnancy. I should've done the full amount of
tests before telling you any diagnostics. I feel
horrible," she said.

"We're all human. We make mistakes.
I've been eating healthy and doing all the
things to make this a healthy pregnancy. I hope
that's what helped the bleeding stop," I said.

She was now rolling the ultrasound instrument around on my stomach. I saw her smile turn into a frown.

"What is it?" I asked.

"There's no heartbeat," she said.

"Maybe try moving it to a different location then," I said.

"There's no baby," she continued.

"You said the test was positive, so I'm confused," I said.

"Ms. Jefferson I'm sorry to inform you but your baby did not make it," she said.

"But you said my test was still positive," I said.

"Yes but that could be because I see some tissues are still present but the fetus is gone. You miscarried," she said.

Kich. A miscarriage. Someone was punishing me.

A part of me died on that table that day. But a small part of me felt at peace. My baby was giving mommy a chance to get it right. But like a dog returns to its vomit I needed to see him. I couldn't feel like I had lost them both.

"Stori let me take you where you have to go. Why are you acting like this?" Brett asked.

"No I'm fine and I want to be alone," I said.

"Can I just take you home then? You don't have to call an Uber," he said.

I left the hospital with him, but I already knew what I was going to do after.

I Ubered to Kich's house. Brett had been calling and texting me non-stop after he dropped me off. I was numb. They sent my prescription that would make the remaining tissues fall out my cervix but honestly they could stay. I didn't care.

I barely stepped onto the front step when Kich came running down.

I fell in his arms.

"Vistoria," Kich carried me in the house.

It normally was a struggle for Kich to carry me but I had lost so much weight from overdosing and now bleeding out an entire baby. My weight had always fluctuated, but lately it was excessive.

Kich was kissing me furiously.

"Don't ever do that to me again. What is wrong with you? You don't know how much I need you," he said as he started trying to take my clothes off.

"I can't Kich," I said.

"If it's your period you know I don't care about that," he said.

"I just miscarried Kich," I said.

He paused.

"Was it mine?" he asked.

He pulled away from me still holding my face.

I wanted to lie to him to stay in his good graces. I loved being here. I didn't want to mess this up, but I know how extensive he was and lying could backfire.

"No," I said.

I looked him directly in his eyes because I wanted to take whatever his punishment was as a woman. If it was a hit, if it was a cursing out, I was going to see it coming.

"Why did you come here?" he asked.

"I can't stand to lose both of you. I can't lose anyone else I love," I said.

"And the father of this baby...do you love him?" he asked.

"No, Kich I only love you," I said.

"What do you need from me tonight Vistoria?" he asked.

"I need you to hold me and show me you love me," I said.

"Come," he said.

He lifted me and carried me to the room. He laid me on his bed. I hadn't felt covers this soft in months.

"Do you need anything? Water, orange juice?" he asked.

"I'll take some juice," I said.

I soon drifted off to sleep and I had the most beautiful dreams.

I woke up the next morning and I thought I was dreaming. Kich was still laying next to me perfect. I inhaled and exhaled the aroma of his house. I missed it here. This was my home. I should've never left. I should've taken whatever came to me that day. We would've healed through it.

"Good morning," Kich said.

He rubbed my hair.

"Vistoria, I love you so much," he said.

"Yes I know," I said.

"And this is why it's going to hurt me to do this. But I can't see you anymore. I can't save you anymore. I can't allow you to break my heart anymore," he said.

"Kich, what do you mean?" I raised up as quick as I could but it was still relatively slow from all the recent abdomen issues.

"Vistoria you got pregnant with another man's baby. At what point did you think I was going to come back for you?" he asked.

"Wow, so now this is all on me? I hadn't heard from you in months. I overdosed. You show up to the hospital and then I don't hear from you again. I thought we were done. So yes, you know me. I went and I had sex with someone. Yes, it was unprotected. And yes, I got pregnant. I didn't love him. He's just someone who made me feel alive when I felt dead after losing you. Kich don't do this to me again. I can't lose you. I can't listen to you say you're giving up on me. I don't deserve this. Lamont and I were only texting and had lunch, but we didn't have sex. We still haven't had sex," I pleaded.

"Vistoria I can't deal with you doing what you want. It physically makes me sick. I am sick at not knowing if you're ok. I am sick at the thought of you loving someone more than me. I can't take you giving them control over you. I can't bear it and I can't keep doing this to myself," he said.

"Kich if there's no us then what do I do? Tell me because I am lost without you. I need direction," I said.

"Go find someone who loves you, get married, have kids, and grow old together," he said.

"How can you tell me to go do things that you know you're gonna hate?" I asked.

"Because this shit doesn't feel any better. Hearing that you were pregnant and miscarried still gave me hope that WE could be a family. But hearing that you miscarried another man's baby is all I can bear. God gave you life but it wasn't my seed. He didn't think to give you my baby and that's a wake up call for me," Kich said.

"How the fuck is that a wake up call when Melanie has never been pregnant," I said.

"As always you speak on things you know nothing about," he said.

"I'll have Rico drop you off. Goodbye Vistoria," he said.

"Kich don't do this," I burst into tears and dropped to my knees.

"Kich please. I'll act right. I'll behave," I said.

"No you won't and that's why I fell in love with you in the 1st place, but I also know toxicity is my familiar. But I'm learning just because I'm ok with it doesn't make it ok," he said as he continued to pull away from me.

Get up Stori. This shit is sad but you will make it through. The Jefferson way. Go 180 the other way.

I kept replaying what Kich said in my head. Each time it played it gave me more strength. It's like I was reprogramming every other command he had ever given me. I eventually was standing. Then I was walking. Then I was going down the stairs.

Find someone who loves you, get married, have kids, and grow old together.

I was leaving out the door and then I was getting in Rico's car.

Find someone who loves you, get married, have kids, and grow old together.

I made it home. I sat on my bed.

Find someone who loves you, get married, have kids, and grow old together.

Lamont

Hey Stori,

I was thinking

about you so I

thought I'd say hi.

I hope we can

move forward

with us again.

But no rush.

Hey Lamont.

We

can.

I'm

ready.

Find someone who loves you, get married, have kids, and grow old together.

Chapter 11

<u>High off Life</u>

My mom was happy to see me doing better. She was exceptionally happy that I was back dating Lamont. I admit the 1st two months I was surprised that Kich still hadn't reached out, but I kept moving forward. What he told me became a mantra in a way. I convinced myself I was doing the right thing. I figured that if I kept working and living like normal people things would be better. I knew when I got pregnant again I would be with a guy who was a family man. I would be with a guy who wasn't traumatized by his past.

Some days were easy and some days were hard but I was making it. I had family all around me and loving me so I would tell myself that was enough. I had always been a strong woman so I knew this was going to pass....eventually. But what didn't pass I would keep suppressing.

Lamont called.

"Hello."

"How are you today?"

"I'm feeling pretty good."

"So how about we get out and grab a bite to eat or maybe go for a walk?"

"That'd be nice."

"Cool and maybe we can catch a movie too. I know you love those."

"I do."

"Well I'll be over in like an hour. Is that enough time?"

"Yep."

"Ok well I'll see you then."

Everything felt weird now. I didn't feel like myself. I felt like I was putting on to appease others. But I refused to spiral back into the state I was in that overdosed. I knew practicing self love was for me. Kich and I had fallen in the worst kind of co-dependent relationship. So the start to my healing was getting back to loving myself. I had to do those things that made me happy. So today it was going to the movies. I knew it was all baby steps. I wasn't going to build the palace in one day, but I sure could lay the stone.

Lamont and I decided to go to dinner and a movie instead.

"What movie are we seeing?" I asked.

"Queen and Slim," he said.

"Oh I haven't seen this preview yet," I said.

Lamont walked around and opened my door.

"Thank you," I said.

He always did everything right.

We were walking to the entrance side by side. He opened the door to the theater. I walked in. He went to purchase our tickets. Lamont was so traditional. Kich would've already had purchased the tickets online.

How am I going to ever get over him?

I suppressed it.

Lamont and I got our popcorn, slushies, and hotdots. We had gotten these same snacks since we were 17.

The movie started and it was so good. And halfway in. I didn't see Lamont and me as Queen and Slim I saw Kich and me.

Suppressed

Bowl of tears.
I drink them.
Swallowed.
Harbored.
Disregarded.
A roaring fire raging.
Boiling, broiling, toiling over.
I can't take it.
I can't shake it.
But I'll erase it.
Erasing what's in pen.
I won't let them in.
Blink.
Once, twice, ten.
Shutter.
Flutter.
Scutter.
Don't let them in.
A fleet on my chest but
I pretend that I'm straight
because that's what resonates.
I love you but I have to sedate
and carry this weight everyday.

The movie ended with me in tears. It was the best movie I had seen in a long time and I truly STANNNED.

"Did you like it?" Lamont asked.

"I loved it," I said.

"I'm glad you did. It feels good to be here with you," he said.

"I'm enjoying this too. It feels good to be out the house," I said.

"Where to now?" he asked.

"We can grab something to eat and head wherever," I said.

We stopped and got food from Zaxby's and headed to Lamont's place.

It was nice. It wasn't Kich's place, but it was simple and well put together.

"You got a new car?" I asked.

"Yeah I've had it for a while I just like to drive old faithful around," he said.

"Oh ok, well it's nice," I said.

I'm not particularly proud of what came from all this but it was inevitable. Lamont was the relationship guy so a few months in he was already saying the M word. It was entirely too soon for me and I didn't even know if that was something I'd ever want to do. I went from living an extravagant life to a simplistic one. I went from dating two people to one. I went from having an open relationship to signing up to be lied to if he ever fucked someone else. But that's what happens in these relationships. If a person has steady income, a car, and a roof over his or her head then it's time for marriage.

I had basically been staying with Lamont now. I had finally got around to picking out my car. It was a Honda Civic that got me where I needed to go. I wanted to pay it off as soon as possible.

I pulled up to my mom's crib to chat with her.

"Hey Pene," I teased.

"Oh you got a man now, a job, and a new car, and suddenly I'm Pene?" she joked.

"So I have something I need advice on," I said.

"Pregnant?" she asked.

"Gosh no Mom," I said.

The thought sent chills down my spine.

"So Lamont has been mentioning marriage lately and I think it may be too fast," I said.

"Too fast...y'all started dating when you were 17 Stori. I don't think it can be too fast," she said.

"Well Mom there were gaps in between that. And we both have dated other people," I said.

"Ok and now y'all are living together doing everything married people do so why not?" she asked.

"Y'all young people confuse me. Y'all do everything a married couple would be doing but have the nerve to question if you should do it," she said.

"Because it's forever," I said.

"Yes it is. But there's also a divorce if it just isn't working," she said.

"Mom," I said shocked that she suggested a divorce.

"Well I never wanted to divorce but look at me and your dad," she said.

"Mom y'all divorced so many years ago I don't know if it counts," I said.

"It still counts. I've always loved him but what we did was needed. God will forgive you. But anyways I don't want to start your marriage with bad omens. You will not get divorced. Stori my entire goal as your mom was to help you create a better life than I had. I know sometimes you feel like I'm trying to force you to do things, but truthfully I'm just doing my best," she said.

"Mom you've done a great job. I don't shun anything you've taught me. It turned me into an amazing person, but I am my own person and that's all I wanted you to see. I wanted you to be proud of me for being me and not just proud of me for being who you wanted me to be," I said.

Things had gotten a whole lot better for me. I had started to master suppression. I cried myself to sleep sometimes when I would visit my mom. I would tell Lamont she needed me, but I just needed to cry and mourn the loss of my last relationship.

Lamont's birthday was coming up. Capricorn. He wanted to go to Prive. The day of Lamont's birthday I knew I had to go all out and be the sexiest thing in there. All his brothers would be there and I wanted everyone to remember I was his trophy bitch and not his fugly first wife. Yes I said FUGLY. Fucking ugly, it wasn't a typo.

Black is always my signature piece. I had on a skin tight black dress that insinuated my curves and I wore my Louboutin heels with a YSL bag Melanie gave me. It was funny that although I was with Lamont this look made me feel like Mrs. Montel.

Find someone who loves you, get married, have kids, and grow old together.

I had gotten my hair done in long, chunky box braids. I looked like someone's Queen. I had my nails done short but in multicolors. That was my thing also.

Lamont looked good as well. He wore a black tailored suit. He had grown his beard out just how I like it, and his stocky shoulders made him look so strong and manly. Lamont always won my heart from his height alone. I love me a 6 feet man. He was the most buff of any guy I've been with.

Well maybe Malroy, but let's focus on relationships here.

"You bout ready to go babe?" he asked.

"Yes," I said.

We walked outside and he hit the automatic start to the car he never drove.

"Oh today is a special day we get to ride in the Chrysler 300," I said.

I smiled. Things meant so much to him because he worked so hard for it. I enjoyed seeing his happiness.

He opened my door for me to get in.

"I'll be right back Stori. I forgot something in the house," he ran back in.

We arrived at Prive. We reserved a more intimate spot in the restaurant. Most of the people called it the "White Room". All of his friends and family were gathered there to support him. I was happy to see him happy.

Find someone who loves you, get married, have kids, and grow old together.

Dinner there was amazing. I ordered the Lobster Bowl and a large garden salad. I was back to my plant-based eating, so I wanted to be sure I had a ton of veggies with my meal. Lamont had the Ribeye and added on a Lobster tail. We definitely were running up a tab, but this was normal to me with Kich.

We all finished our meals, and bottle girls came out holding a cake with sparkles burning. I wasn't sure if Prive did this. I was zoning out so much that I didn't notice the banner one of the bottle girls was holding.

I was just smiling and looking at Lamont trying to hold everything together.

I probably shouldn't have eaten an entire edible before going there but hey.

Lamont got out of his seat and bent to tie his shoe.

I was wondering why it was so urgent for him to tie his shoe. I was still smiling and looking at everyone.

"Stori, Vistoria....will you?" he asked.

"Will I what babe?" I responded.

My fucking high is blown..what the fuck does that sign say?

There was a glitch in the system. I froze. I stopped breathing.

Find someone who loves you, get married, have kids, and grow old together.

Find someone who loves you, get married, have kids, and grow old together.

He's asking me to marry him. You knew this was coming. Snap the fuck out of it. Even if you don't want to you have to say yes it's his birthday.

What the fuck did you think would come from this dumb ass? Oh you thought he was a Kich where y'all could live free lives with no attachments. Lamont is a family guy. A marriage guy. You know the same one who married a whole other bitch before you.

Find someone who loves you, get married, have kids, and grow old together.

I could see worry starting to come across his face and others. They were recording this.

I am being recorded looking like a bump on a fucking log.

You've been recorded doing worst shit bitch. Yes or No hoe?

"Yes, yes, I will," I jumped down into his arms.

Dumb bitch.

"I was starting to get worried there for a second," he whispered in my ear.

"I'll tell you in the car," I said.

After everything died down and hours of hugging people and congratulations we were finally getting back in the car. We left the house as boyfriend and girlfriend and we were headed back as fiancés.

"So is now a good time to discuss why you took so long to answer? I was starting to think you wouldn't," Lamont asked.

"Babe, I'm just high as fuck and now thanks to you I'm high off life," I said.

Chapter 12
<u>Through sickness</u>

Through sickness and health. Yep...you read that right. A few months in Lamont proposed. It still felt forced. But at this point I felt robotic. I felt like the girl at the beginning of this story. I felt like I wasn't living a life that was my own. I felt like I was living a life for other people.

"Have you decided where you want to start your dress shopping at?" Kara asked.

"David's Bridal I guess," I said.

"Stori are you going to give me any enthusiasm? You are ruining this for me," she whined.

"Kara you know I'm not into all this," I said.

"All this. Your wedding? Your marriage? You only do this once...maybe twice but still. You aren't taking any of this serious," she barked.

"Do maid of honors have to be more stressed out than the bride cause if so you're doing amazing sweetie?" I joked.

"I'm glad you can laugh but I can't. If things look bad they won't judge you. No, they will judge me," she said.

"Ok Kara, so where do you want me to go?" I asked.

I was trying to listen to her plea although I truly didn't care. Lamont and I could've went to the courthouse which I told him. But he had a savings account specifically for this, his parents did, and my parents did. Although I'm sure my dad's contribution was rather small. My dad was cheap and after marrying my mom vowed to never marry again. I was surprised that he was supportive of me getting married, but he didn't give any pushbacks. Well he didn't give me any issues, but I'm sure my dad could find a reason to bitch with my mom. Either way I was glad that they didn't bring any of the drama to me. These days most of my family and friends tried to keep any uproar away from me for fear that I would relapse.

"So I have a list of shops we need to hit. We need to find the perfect dress to accentuate your boobs and bum without looking slutty," she said.

"Uh huh. So how many shops are you going to drag me to?" I asked.

"Only like 5. It will go by fast and you don't have to get done in one day. We have plenty of time. The wedding can't go on until the bride has her dress right?" she asked.

"I suppose you're right," I said.

So 5 shops turned into 20. The next few weeks were spent picking the perfect dress for Kara. She had a vision in her head and I had to allow my bestie to live it.

"So the dress we picked today was perfect right?" she asked.

"Custom made Cinderella dress that

transforms into the perfect reception dance dress," she gloated.

"I'm very excited with our outcome. It took a lot of stores to get it, but I am happy," I said.

"That's because they wanted you in a dress that was already made. No, this is original. The way you're gonna go from Cinderella at 11:59 to Cinderella at midnight by choice will be captivating. You will twirl and I will bibbidi-bobbidi boo you," she said.

"Well the bibbidi actually …," she cut me off.

"Shush! Don't you dare overanalyze this and take my starring moment away," she said.

"Now let me finish. I will bibbidi-bobbidi boo and the Cinderella bottom will fall to pieces and out you will pop looking sexier than ever in a Wilma Flintstone fit and yesss we will all stan," she said.

"I am grateful for the stanning," I said.

"Stori this moment makes me extremely happy. You should be. You thought you had lost Lamont once and look at how things have come full circle. But never forget I support you," she grabbed my hands.

"I support you in whatever decision you make. If you say this isn't what you want we can leave it all right now and cancel everything. I will save all these plans for when you do walk down that aisle. I know you. And this could be the, "Stori doesn't want the glam and party" scenario or "Stori knows she's making a mistake but doing it anyways". And more than anything I want you to know I have your back. You don't have to do this," she said.

"But dont I? Kich and I are over. I'm only getting older. Lamont is a good catch and this is just what people do," I said.

"Some things may be what people do but we know everything isn't what you do," she said.

"Thank you," I said.

"It's never too late. I just want you to be happy no matter what that may be," she said.

That night I went to bed thinking about what Kara had said.

Why does life throw so many hard decisions?

My maid of honor called me to make sure I was ready for my bridal shower. I got to escape the engagement party, but she said this one was a necessity because all I had to do was show up and collect gifts. If anything I was ready for my bachelorette party because I wanted to see strippers. I heard I could even get gifts then, but they would be sex oriented.

Kara

"Are you ready bitch?"

"Kara, you act like we're going somewhere extravagant. It's just a meetup with people I know. Some I like and some I don't. It's not that big of a deal."

"Stori, can you let me have this? It's not everyday that my best friend gets married."

"I know. But you know parties and stuff aren't my thing. My social anxiety flares up."

"You will be ok. I'll be there."

"Kara that doesn't make me feel any better you are a social butterfly."

"OMG, I can tell from this convo that you aren't even dressed. I'm coming over and we're getting dressed together."

I don't know how she knew it, but I definitely wasn't dressed.

I sat there when Kara and I got off the phone just looking at myself in the mirror. Then I heard a knock on the door.

"Girl you still up here sitting in that chair naked?" Lamont asked.

"Yes I know. I still haven't moved. I am horrible," I said.

"What time are you heading to the bridal shower? You gots to get them gifts girl," he joked.

"I mean can't you just get them for me?" I asked.

"I don't think it works that way," he said.

"A few of my sisters and cousins will get there soon. My mom said she won't be able to make it, but she sent her gifts with them," he said.

"That's fine. Maybe a few more people will cancel," I said.

"Book, you're gonna have to get over this one day," he said.

"Yeah I know. I just don't see why people are so big on parties. Every single thing is a celebration. Most of us don't even know what we're celebrating we just do it. Most holidays are pagan, but we still do it. Did you know the act of blowing out candles itself is pagan? People believed that by blowing the candles out the smoke would carry their prayers to the gods and goddesses," I rambled.

"Are you done?" he asked.

"Nope," I said.

"I love when you get like this. You're so cute when you're ranting," he kissed my forehead.

His kiss triggered a heartbeat down below. I opened my mouth and inhaled slowly. I pressed my lips together. I let the sensation go through me. Then I cracked my mouth and exhaled.

"Look at you," he said.

I smiled.

"I gotta get dressed. I can't be in here playing with you," I said.

It had been a while since Lamont and I had sex. I think in a way we were waiting it out for our wedding night. You know to kinda make it special. I wanted to get it on right then and there. But I knew I had people waiting for me. Lamont had that look in his eyes and I was trying to ignore it.

I knew it was going to go down.

Fuck the wedding.

Lamont grabbed me and placed me on my dresser. He spread my legs and started to lick. I loved Lamont's full lips. He had lips that were the same on the top and bottom. So when he tasted me his lips always gripped my entire vagina in his mouth. I gasped.

"Ahhh shit," I said.

He put his middle and pointer finger in my mouth. He moved them in and out as he continued to eat me. The act sent shocks throughout my body.

I was cumming in no time.

"Fuckkkkkkkkk," I moaned as I burst all over him.

"Come fuck me," I said.

"You gotta wait for that when you get back," he said.

Lamont loved eating pussy. He could eat me out for hours before fucking me. I loved that about him. That's one area he never slacked in. Honestly, Lamont was probably my favorite pussy eater. He would eat it anywhere and in any way.

"Oh so you're a big tease," I said as I started to put my clothes on.

I threw on a cute white dress. It was form fitting with sleeves. I paired it with a gold Sam Edelman heel. I wasn't in the mood to overdress so earrings, necklaces, and any ring other than my engagement one was left off. I knew Kara was going to take one look at me and be appalled but hey.

I addded some lipgloss and waited for her to get there. When she arrived we were already running so late that she didn't bitch at me.

"Girl just get in. I can't even fuss at you about this lack of face you have right now. I should've known when you text me that you were dressed and that I didn't have to help you that it was a lie and you needed help," she fussed.

"Sorry," I said.

"Yo ass aint sorry," she said.

We pulled up to the venue and there were so many cars outside. I could feel my anxiety growing, but I knew it would pass once I got inside. It's like I had to face it, be in it, and then I could deal.

We played a ton of games. I think one of my favorites was watching my friends and family make wedding dresses from toilet paper.

We ate delicious finger foods and drank mimosas and more. It was almost perfect until we decided to go off schedule and just have girl talk.

"So when do you and my brother plan to have babies?" one of his sisters asked.

"Well I don't know exactly. Let's get through the wedding 1st," I tried to joke although the topic sent a sour taste in my mouth.

"Do you know how many you want to have?" she continued.

"I'll have as many as God blesses me with," I said.

Kara knew this topic wasn't a good one for me so she attempted to change the subject.

"So who wants to help me carry these gifts to the car?" Kara asked.

A few volunteered but it was like this particular sister had it out for me.

"I'm just ready to be an auntie so I'm hoping you guys get busy soon," she continued.

"What's your name again? I forgot which sister you are," I said.

"Shelley," she said.

"Ohhhh. Shelley. Don't you have like 5 kids of your own? Does it matter if I have 1 or 2?" I said.

Kara just started to distribute gifts into people's hands because this was going left.

"Did I offend you?" she asked.

"I just want you to worry more about your pussy and less about mine," I said.

"And there it goes," Kara said.

"Ok everyone, take any leftovers and decorations that you see. Take a gift to the car. But the shower is over," Kara said.

"So now I see," she said.

"See what?" I asked.

"Why he dated you years ago but you weren't his 1st wife," she said.

"Ohh wow. So we're going there?" I asked.

"You've never got a ring. You're his only sister that isn't married," I said.

At this point his sisters had formed a side and my friends and cousins had.

"Say the word and I'll spray this entire place," Cookie said.

"So how'd the shower go?" Lamont asked.

"Great. I can't wait to be apart of the family," I said as I got undressed and prepared for bed. I was so glad I wouldn't have to see them again until the wedding. None of them were invited to my bachelorette party. That was for me and my girls to let loose and have fun. No one who would snitch or cockblock would be invited. I had anticipated this moment longer than I did the wedding. I always wanted to be the female version of the "Hangover".

Lamont apologized on behalf of his sister. Although he didn't know the reason why her question triggered me. I just had complications with a pregnancy, so what she asked sent me over the edge.

I'd be lying if I didn't say the horrid bridal shower didn't have me rethinking marrying Lamont. I was going to be marrying into his family, and I'm sure they hated me. My thoughts of uncertainty birthed thoughts of Kich. It was like he was calling out to me telepathically. I needed his energy around me and within me. I missed him and on this night suppression wasn't helping.

Succubus
I knew you in a past life.
I don't remember our past strifes.
I could've been your past wife.
But in this present life I'm accepting
whatever you're giving.
I'm taking your poison within me.
Give me your chaotic noise and unsettling.
Your aggression so tantalizing.
Romanticism you win the prize in.
Sapiosexual fucking my mind's gems.
How do you own me
when we haven't touched?
How are you in me
yet we haven't fucked?
I feel your aura.
You sense my pheromones.
Give me your energy.
I want to suck your soul.

     It was Kara's idea for us to go to Vegas. I was so happy to see all my girls: Cookie, Kara, Rama. A part of me wanted to invite Melanie. I even felt I was wrong for not inviting her. We fussed, fought, and fucked so she had a part of my heart. But I knew there was no way in hell Kich would let her attend a bachelorette party of me marrying another guy.

I hadn't seen Rama in a very long time. When I moved in with Kich and she went back to Atlanta we didn't keep in touch much.

Kara, Cookie, and I flew into Vegas together and Rama flew in from ATL. Kara and Cookie could've flown in from ATL being that they still lived there. However, they were in Memphis so much with Cookie's boo being there, and Kara started coming around more after my suicide attempt. I guess she felt bad because as an Aquarius she had zoned out on me and hadn't realized how bad I was doing at the time. It worked out because we all were from this area so we had friends and family around when it was necessary.

"Rama!" I said as I ran to the baggage claim area.

Rama's flight was a straight shot from ATL so she got there hours before us.

"I've missed you so much," I said as I squeezed her really tight.

"I miss you too. It's been forever since I saw you," she said.

"I know, forgive me. You left here after Kich's party and my life got kind of crazy. I could've kept in touch so much better," I apologized.

"Stori. Heart to heart later. Grab your luggage now," Kara reminded me.

"Oh shit," I turned and studied the converyor belt.

I saw my multi-color Mia Toro luggage coming around.

"That's me," I said as I jolted my bag towards me.

Cookie and Kara already had their bags. I didn't realize I was the hold up.

"Uber XL or wait for a shuttle?" I asked.

"We can do the Uber. I don't feel like waiting for a shuttle," Cookie said.

"Uber it is. I'll do it," I replied.

We got the Uber and arrived at our destination. Kara knew how to make me smile. She had us booked for the Paris Las Vegas hotel. We had the St.Tropez room and it was magnificent. It had a separate living room that was very large and needed for the festivities. Also the dining area and sleeping area were separate. It was like a small piece of Paris and its atmosphere. I loved all the custom accent pieces and décor. The chandeliers glistened above.

For a moment, I forgot why I was there and with whom. It was grand, it was Kich. I inhaled and exhaled. I couldn't remember my mantra. I was starting to panic. Why was I doing this? Why was I here? Who was I kidding? I fucking needed him.

I sat down at the nearest table.

"Stori are you ok?" Kara asked.

"Yes," I tried to find something to switch the topic.

"Where's Cook?" I asked.

"Oh girl you know her and her antics couldn't stay with us. She booked a room on another level. Ms. Bougie needed her own space," she said.

"Oh girl, Cook need that room for more than just space," I laughed.

I had detoured Kara and myself.

"Can we turn some music on?" I asked.

"Hell yea! I brought my speaker too," Kara said.

"You guys are always prepared," Rama said.

"When it comes to having a good time Kara is always prepared. Now if this was something else...don't bank on it," I joked.

"Oh fuck you. I choose what I want to care about that's all," she said.

"So what are we listening to?" Rama asked.

"Bitch this is Yo Gotti! The Memphis

legend himself," Kara hissed.

"Sorry," Rama apologized.

"Girl ignore her. She's very serious about her music," I said.

"So what you been up to?" I asked.

"Talk and drink," Kara said.

"Girl how did you fix this drink that fast?" I asked.

"Don't worry bitch drink," she commanded.

I drank and continued talking to Rama.

"Rama when did you get a twin?" I asked.

I could hear Kara burst into laughter.

"Takara! What did you give me?" I forced the words out of my mouth.

"I might have added a pill or two in the champagne," she said.

"Takara. Why would you do that?" I screamed.

"So we can have a damn good time. This trip is expensive as fuck and I'll be damned if it's not the best," she said.

"We could've had a good time sober," I said.

"Have you seen y'all boring asses sober?" she asked.

"This was a bad idea. What are we gonna do if we're all fucked up?" I asked.

"Oh we won't all be. I gave you and

Rama two. I have one and Cookie won't have any because she threatened me already," she said.

"I should've threatened you," I said.

"Oh it'll be fine. The party is coming to us. We have no reason to leave the hotel room," she said.

There was more drinking, more drugs, and more people. At some point I don't remember inviting all of them. I knew some of them were strippers but some were strangers. It didn't matter. We were in Vegas having the time of our lives. Until it hit me.

I was getting fucking married in a week.

A fucking week!!!!

And there it went....

I was sobbing in a corner when Kara found me.

"Bitch...what is wrong?" she asked.

"I'm making a mistake," I said.

"I have to get Kich back," I said.

But this is what Kich wanted. If there is no Kich then I can't pass up on Lamont. Lamont is here and ready. He is my 1st love. I am doing the right thing. I can't risk losing Lamont and Kich. I will not end up alone with some fucking cats.

"Stori, talk to me. Do you feel like you're marrying the wrong man?" she asked.

I heard her talking but my replies were

locked in my brain.

Kich is everything I don't need. We are just soul tied and he is roaming around in my psyche. That doesn't mean we are meant to be. That just means we are joined by our toxicity. He doesn't fucking deserve me.

These were things I tried to convince myself of knowing I was at fault. The only thing I could blame Kich for was dating multiple women, but he didn't do that in secret. I was the liar. I broke the levels of trust.

"I see your eyes moving. I see your lips looking like you want to respond, but you aren't saying anything," she said.

I wanted to run to Kich, but I knew I couldn't. We were done and he hated me. Maybe it wasn't hate, but he wanted nothing to do with me.

Waited Again

I'm back here again.
My heart can't pretend
that I don't love you.
Because I do.
It hurts because I waited for you.
I didn't learn my lesson the first time.
You broke up with me a year ago
you'd think I'd be fine.
I can't let it go.
I can't let you go.
You don't come out.
Please, I could've waited
for you forever.
But forever seemed so far away
whenever you would say
we're never getting back together.
I should be happy.
I should be glad.
You say you don't need me.
You say I was nothing to be had.
You lied to yourself
convincing your heart
of how I was wrong.
But you didn't see my worth
because I was an object
to be owned.

Strippers came to the room and it was a joy. There were male and female strippers, so I was getting my entire life.

The next morning I woke up with pussy on my breath and I couldn't remember who it belonged to.

I think it was Rama but it could've been the stripper with the perky tits like Melanie.
Oh wait, I do remember how sweet she tasted.
I wanted to do this since we met.

My memory was really shot that's how bad I got fucked up.

I was still high but I was functioning. I grabbed my phone to see how Lamont's night went.

I'm sure they got wild too.

He and his friends were in Cali for his bachelor festivities. I had told him he could just come to Vegas, but he insisted on us enjoying ourselves apart. Which after the night I had I was happy for that.

I got my phone. I had 50 missed calls from Kich.

What the fuck?

Chapter 13
<u>Marry</u>

I crawled on the floor and out into the hall. Somewhere in my brain I thought this was a top secret mission. I picked up my phone to call Kich back and he was calling again.

Kich

"Hey..."

"Vistoria!"

I heard him take a deep breath.

"Yes I'm here."

"What are you thinking?"

"Kich I don't remember anything we talked about last night. Kara gave me all kinds of drugs and drinks."

"You're getting married?"

"Kich...yes. That's what you told me to do."

"I did. I didn't know it would hurt so bad hearing you say it."

"Kich I can't take this now. You can't do this now. I get married in a week."

"Vistoria you're not getting married."

He laughed.

"Kich there are plans. There is money spent. I accepted a man's proposal."

"I'll refund every dollar spent from my own pocket."

"Kich you think this makes it easier for me?"

"Vistoria who do you need? Who gives you the will to live? Who lights up every atom in your body? If you tell me it's him then I will leave. But if it's not. The wedding is off. I'm coming to get you."

"Kich what are people going to think? I turn down a good man a week before our wedding to get back with my throuple."

"Please don't call us a throuple. You know there's no limit on who or how many we love. The restraints in that make me want to throup-up."

"Kich how are you joking at a time like this? I am a literal mess now."

"You're a mess because you're more worried about what people will say than your own happiness. Fuck them."

"It's not that easy and you know it's not

that easy."

"It's going to be harder if I have to drag your ass off the altar. So if I were you I would save a lot of people some time and energy and just come home now. You're in Vegas at which hotel again? I'm leaving in an hour."

"Kich don't come here."

"Would you rather me wait for you to arrive home and show up outside?"

"Kich what can I do to make you stop this?"

"Say you don't love me more than any other guy you've been with."

"I don't know if this is love Kich. It feels more like control."

"You're stalling. I'll see you when I get to Vegas."

End call.

I spread out like the Vitruvian Man on the floor staring at the ceiling.
What the fuck am I gone do now?
Do I hide from Kich? Do I press

charges and get a restraining order?

Why are you acting as if this isn't what you really want? He's saving you.

But I'm going to look like a bad person to so many people. So many gifts, so many plans.

He said he would refund any expenses and you know he got it. If I were you I'd cancel now while people can get refunds. The day of will be more hectic because some things just can't be refunded then.

Are you seriously considering leaving a good man like Lamont for Kich?

But what makes Lamont ….good?

When Kara found me I was still spread eagle on the carpet staring at the ceiling while my thoughts battled one another. When I was a kid I named them Possiana and Negula. As I've grown older I've realized Negula was just real as fuck. She gave me my raw truth no matter how ugly it was. She made me look at situations for what they were and not what I wanted them to be.

"Stori, should I be worried?" she asked.

"Yes, you should be petrified," I said as I rolled over.

"Ok maybe I gave you too much," she said with regret.

"No it wasn't your roofies. It's Kich," I said.

"What happened?" she sat on the carpet

with me.

"Bitch, Kich says he's coming and will be here within the next few hours," I said.

She burst out laughing.

"I must fucking say that nigga is dysfunctional as fuck but I stan," she said.

"Kara! What kind of support is that?" I asked.

"I'm just saying," she said.

"Kara he told me he didn't want me anymore," I said.

"And you believed him?" she asked.

"Yes. Are you forgetting everything that's happened since we broke up over me texting someone else," I said.

"No bitch, don't be slick now. You were texting your 1st love, in his house, on the phone bill he pays, and his internet. And then yo' hoe ass kept it a secret," she said.

"Wow, thanks for the support," I griped.

"If you want a yes man you better befriend one of them bitches who scared of you," she said.

I rolled my eyes.

"So do you think I'm making a mistake with Lamont?" I asked.

"Stori, I've said this before. Only you can choose and whatever you choose I'm 100% behind you," she said.

I lied down on her and exhaled.

So this is where social media can get you killed if it was dropped in the hands of the wrong person.

"He can come to Vegas, but he won't know where we are," I said.

"Well," Kara said.

"What the fuck did you do Kara?" I asked.

"I tagged our hotel when I was telling people to pull up last night," she said.

"Well Kich probably didn't watch it. Go delete it real quick," I said.

Kara picked up her phone and headed to IG.

"Yeah...Kich Mawni watched it," she said.

"You sure it's his personal account and not a fan account or something?" I asked.

"Blue check mark...it's him," she said.

Kich watched Kara's IG story and found out we were at the Paris Las Vegas. And it's no shocker that Kich had access to every fucking thing because he got the Napoleon Suite.

This is where shit gets crazy. Ok, it's been crazy. This is where shit gets crazier. Kara and I get up and go into the room to bathe. I was doing that thing we women do where we convince ourselves he isn't getting any pussy yet we do everything to be sure "she's" in tip-top shape. The St.Tropez had a deep, spa tub and a shower. I got in the tub just in case something popped off with Kich and I needed to be on point.

Yes I fucking know I'm engaged, but what the fuck do you expect me to do? Get Kich arrested?

I got some sugar from the coffee area and took it in the bathroom with me. I scrubbed my lips with that and some coconut oil I had brought. I also used it to scrub my feet . I had a little left so I did the rest of my body. This would make me all soft.

I frowned at the fact that I was an engaged woman prepping for my ex to visit me.

There's seriously something wrong with you. You can mess up any good thing.

I got out the tub and got dressed. I put on a red tank top dress that was very fitting to my curves. I wore my red Converses instead of the cute little sandals I originally had planned. I didn't know if I would have to fight Kich or something crazy.

"What time are we heading to the Eiffel Tower thing?" I asked.

"It's like 12 something now, so probably around 1:30 or 2 if everyone is dressed," she said.

"Ok, well I'm about to go down to the lobby and get something to snack on," I said. I grabbed my red GG Marmont matelassé leather belt bag and threw the room key inside.

I headed out the room and to the elevator. I got to the lobby level and opened the elevator and stepped out. As I stepped out, there he was, checking in...Kich.

I turned around quickly and hit the button so the elevator could come back. I peeked and he was still at the desk. The elevator came back and I stepped inside. As I turned to push the close door button he was turning away from the desk. The look on his face was rage and admiration. My heart was racing.

This is Kich. Why are you acting as if he's a murderer?

Well I don't know that he isn't.

The elevator opened up and I was nervous as fuck. I could barely get my room key out. My hands were trembling. I pulled the key from my bag and started to put it into the door.

"Vistoria..Princess...why are you doing this? Are you afraid of me now?" Kich said as he was getting off the elevator. His voice was getting closer and closer.

"You should be running to me, but you're running away. I can't tell you how much that hurts me," he said.

I could feel his breath on my neck although he hadn't made it to me yet.

I finally got the door open and Kich had a hand full of my braids.

"Vistoria what am I going to do with you?" he said as he pushed me through the door into the room.

Rama was on the couch on her phone and Kara was walking out the bathroom from doing her makeup.

"Ohhh hey Kich," she said.

"Let me go," I said.

"Vistoria don't make this any harder on you than it has to be," he said.

I tried to go the opposite way from Kich and he continued pulling me by my hair.

"Come on let's go in the room and talk," he said.

"Kara! You're not going to help me? You're gonna let him do this to me?" I yelled.

"Girl that's between y'all. Let me know if he hits you," she joked.

"Kich let my fucking hair go. I hate you. I hate you. You make me sick. I'm sick of you. You think you can leave me and pick me up when you want. I hate you, you fucking piece of shit," I yelled as Kich used his strength to overpower me. For a guy who was 5'9" maybe 190-200 pounds he felt like a bulldozer. I couldn't even ground my feet,

"Rama? So no one thinks this is too far?" I yelled before Kich pushed me in the room and slammed the door.

Once we got inside he released my hair and put his hands around my neck.

"Kneel," he said.

"No! Fuck you," I said and I spit in his face.

I don't know what color comes after black but I felt like Kich's eyes did that. It's like they went black and red.

He threw me onto the bed and climbed on top of me.

"You think you no longer belong to me? Have you tricked your brain? He poked me on my temples. Let me in," he said.

"You're psychotic you know that?" I said sarcastically.

"You will be kneeling and apologizing by the time I'm done with you," Kich said.

He kept one hand around my neck and used his legs to pry mine open. Once he had them apart he shoved his fingers inside me.

"Ouch," I said.

"I hate you. I hate you," I kept saying.

"Shut the fuck up," he said as he shoved his fingers deeper inside me.

I could feel my body responding to him, but I wasn't giving in. I was enraged and tired of him thinking he owned me.

"Smell that," he took his fingers out and put them to my nose.

"Your pheromones have told off on you. You want me and you want me bad. I started taking it too nice on you, never again. You will always know your place. You aren't going anywhere, you aren't getting married to anyone, all that shit is canceled," he said.

I could hear him unbuttoning his pants.

"No I don't want to. I'm engaged Kich. This isn't right," I said.

Bitch, you prepped for this. Shut yo' dramatic ass up.

I'm gonna feel so guilty.

He thrust himself into me.

I gasped out. It all came back into me. I cannot describe it. It was like a lock and key. I immediately burst into tears.

"Why would you leave me? Why would you make me feel like you didn't love me? Why would you? I would die for you. I would give my life for you. I would sell my soul for you and you just left me. You never gave me a chance. You threw me away," I cried.

He pulled out during all my tears flowing and zipped up his pants.

He stood up.

"What are you doing? Why did you stop?" I asked.

"Don't leave me Kich I can't take it," I jumped up and into his arms.

"Kneel," he said.

I kneeled.

"Look up at Daddy," he said.

I looked up.

"Open your mouth," he said.

I opened my mouth.

He spit in my mouth.

And just like that I was back.

"You want me to fuck you?" he asked.

"Yes please," I said.

"No," he said.

"I'm gonna go to my room. Go out and enjoy your day. I will summon you when I want to see you," he said.

"I'm sorry," I said.

He put his hands up to my lips.

"You belong to me. You are mine. I am you and you are me. When I hurt you, I was only hurting myself. Nothing you've done requisites an apology. I am responsible for you. I should've never left you or made you feel like you had to leave. I will never make you feel unsafe again. There's nothing you can ever do to make me not love you. I don't love the idea of you. I don't love the feeling of you. I love you without conditions," he said.

I had melted. I can't express the way Kich's words hit me.

He exited the bedroom and I was still on my knees watching him walk away. I heard him exit the suite.

Kara and Rama both ran in the room.

"Are you okay?" Rama asked.

"Bitch...you back sprung," Kara said.

I couldn't even speak.

I sat on the bed.

"Earth to fucking Stori," Kara said.

"What am I gonna do. How can I marry Lamont after that?" I asked.

Chapter 14
<u>Good Person</u>

I tried to continue my day as normal as possible. I was between a rock and a sadistic. I had no idea how to move forward. I wanted to post pics to the gram of me having a good time in Vegas. However, it all seemed stupid when I had basically just fucked another man days before I got married. I loved Lamont with so much of my heart. I mean hell I was in love with Lamont, but Kich was different. I wish I could draw you a picture of my heart. Lamont was in my heart...buried in there. Lamont could never lose his place in my heart. But Kich was my entire fiber of being. Kich was my reason for breathing. I know they say you aren't supposed to love someone this much because it's toxic and unhealthy. We are that and we don't care. I'm not a good person. I want to be a good person. I've tried to be a good person, but I'm not. Kich gets that. Kich doesn't try to make me be good. Kich just lets me be me. I had the toughest decision to make and I knew it wouldn't be easy. I knew it would come at a cost. Someone was going to be hurt. But ultimately I had to do what was best for me.

So how do I choose? Do I choose the man who I want to be or do I choose the man I am?

Twin Flame
You left my heart on the floor.
Instead of picking it up
you crushed it once more.
What did I ever do to you that
brought this from your core?
You point the finger at me and
say it was I who 1ˢᵗ tore.
All I ever tried to do was love you
when loving you was hard.
You didn't make it easy.
I wasn't given an award.
I received no praise for all the
things I did right.
So,so many tears cried
on so many nights.
Wondering why I wasn't your pick.
Maybe love just isn't enough
and that explains it.
I just needed you to care
when so much in my life
filled me with despair.
Does crushing me build your ego?
Or does it make your issues seem low?
Because there are many.
Flaws...we have plenty.
I'm the one to blame for
causing us so much pain.
Broken mirror images that remain.
Whether we end it all together or strain.
I'll die knowing I lived my twin flame.

My brain was racing all while we toured the Eiffel Tower. I pushed through to not be a pooper, but I was somewhere in outer space. All I wanted to do was make Kich happy and not crush Lamont. I had no idea how this was even possible.

You really messed up this time Stori.

The lines were pretty long but that was beneficial for me. I could zone out and not seem like it since it was a lot of waiting.

"Stori," Kara said.

"Yeah I heard you," I said.

"Well we're next," she said.

I had zoned out so much I didn't realize our wait was over.

I guess this worked for your good.

Not funny.

When we got to the top it was absolutely beautiful. We could see all of Vegas and I felt on top of the world. We took a ton of selfies although it was extremely windy. I was glad we all had hairstyles that wouldn't go anywhere. Rama and Kara were au natural and I had braids.

In my attempt to be normal I went ahead and posted a cute picture on IG. I was looking bomb as fuck in my red fit. I had to spruce up a bit after my Kich interaction, but nonetheless I was still a baddie.

I put my phone down because I didn't want to stalk the likes. We were headed to go eat and I picked it back up.

Zayphillips started following you.

Here the fuck we go. Just what I needed. Of all the fucking days. Like what the fuck? Why do they come in two's when they come?

zayphillips
How you been?
storitime
Engaged.
zayphillips
Congrats.
storitime
Thanks.

Yes. Bitch. I moved the fuck on.

zayphillips
To Kich?

Oh...look at this toxic Scorpio tryna sting me. He knows damn well I'm not engaged to Kich. Kich doesn't do marriage because he can't marry more than one person here.

storitime
No.

zayphillips
Well congrats to you and the lucky guy I've thought of you a few times.
storitime
That's cool. Well I hope you enjoy your day.

I was a little shocked that Zay wrote me after all this time but then I wasn't. He's a Scorpio so he will always want to feel like he has control. I hope he sees that he doesn't. I'm out here engaged. He completely lost. Move on. It's funny how a man I was once crazy about was now a memory. My body didn't crave him anymore. I would have to open it up to him for it to crave him. That's how Kich was different. I never stopped craving Kich.

I couldn't be worried about Zay when I had this Kich situation growing inside of me like a tumor.

We stayed up there for a good bit of time taking photos, and we even watched the Bellagio fountain show. Everything was even prettier as the sun started to set.
I did it. I convinced them I'm not a total hot mess right now.
Barely.
So as we descended from the Eiffel Tower I received a text from Kich.
Sometimes I feel like he has a tracker

on me.

Kich

Come to me.

On my way.

"Where do you guys want to eat at?" Rama asked.

"Where the fuck is Cook?" Kara asked.

"Girl you already know," I laughed.

We all laughed.

We made it back into the hotel.

"When y'all decide where you wanna eat hit me up. I'm about to step away for a bit," I said.

"Step away my ass. I'm ordering room service and I'm putting it on Kich's tab. Tell him to approve it," Kara said as we got in the elevator.

"Sure bitch," I said.

Things immediately change with Kich. Some things just aren't an issue with him.

I made it to his suite. I knocked on the door and waited for him to open it.

"Thank you for knocking," he said.

"Certainly," I said with my bowed head.

"May I enter?" I asked.

"Yes you may," he said.

"Lift your head Stori. I want to see your face," he said.

Kich's suite was way different from

ours. It had 3 bedrooms and five bathrooms. Of course Kich had a grand piano in his room because apparently that's a necessity of his now.

I walked closely behind Kich waiting for him to give me instructions. I had no idea what he was going to do to me.

We walked to the wet bar area and Kich went behind to fix drinks.

"You can sit," he said.

I found the nearest chair and sat down. The décor in Kich's suite was a deep red with gold accents all over. It truly gave a royalty feel.

"Are we having drinks?" I asked.

"You didn't ask permission to speak," he said.

"Sorry," I said.

"Try again," he said.

"May I have permission to speak?" I asked.

"No, I don't want to hear your voice right now. I want to look at you," he said.

"Stand up," he said.

I stood up.

"Take off that dress," he said.

I started to pull the dress up to take it over my head.

"Not like that. Pull it back down," he said.

I pulled the dress back down.

"Peel it off your body," he said.

"Take one strap, then the next, and so on and so forth," he said.

I slowly picked up my left strap with my right hand and tipped it off my shoulder.

"Yes," Kich said.

His black eyes were piercing my body.

I took my left hand and eased the right strap off. Then I slowly pulled my arm out of the strap and did the other side. I used both hands to pull the dress down near my boob area. I continued pulling down the dress, over my stomach, over my plump ass, around my thighs, down to my knees, and then I dropped it to my ankles.

"Step out of it," he said.

I stepped out the dress.

"Now your bra," he said.

I took my hands behind my back and unclasped my bra. I then took my right hand and stripped off the left strap. I proceeded to strip off the right strap with my left hand. I held the bra in my hands pushed against my boobs.

"Drop it," he said.

I dropped it to the floor.

"Thong," he said.

I grabbed each side of my thong and rolled them down my legs.

"Step out," he said.

"Bend over," he demanded.

I bent over.

"Take your hands and spread your cheeks," he said.

"Bend more," he said.

I was now bent with my head near my ankles while spreading my cheeks.

"That pink perfect pussy," he said.

He walked over and welted my pussy with his tongue.

I moaned.

"Shut the fuck up. Didn't I say I didn't want to hear you. Do you think this is for your pleasure? This is for me. Put this in your slutty ass mouth," Kich pulled a gag from his pocket.

He whisked me around and put it in my mouth.

"Ask me your question from earlier," he said.

I asked although now my mouth was gagged and the words were muffled.

"Are.... we.... hav..ing.. drinks? I forced out.

"Here," he grabbed a bottle of Don Julio and poured it over my face.

"You can have a little to drink but that's it. No getting high and not remembering all the ways I'm going to fuck you tonight. You will remember me completely. By the time I am done you won't know what another man looks like," he said.

I swallowed the fragments of tequila

that drizzled into my mouth.

I knew it was going to be a long night.

Kich picked me up and carried me into the master bedroom. He plopped me on the bed and went to the desk and grabbed a pack of Okamoto condoms.

I started crying because I felt so low like Kich now saw me as trash. He had never used a condom with me.

"Vistoria crying won't stop anything that I do to you tonight," he said.

"Get on all fours and arch your back bitch," he said.

I did as I was told.

He put the condom on and threw the paper near my head.

He then entered me and moaned.

"Ahhh, it's still tight. Looks like you haven't been too much of a whore," he said.

"I might actually be disappointed," he said.

He started spanking me as he went in and out. He spread my cheeks and pounded me. Then he took it from my pussy and into my ass. He didn't bother using any lube.

I screamed out.

"Do I wanna hear you?" he asked.

"No.... sir," I said.

I was just happy he put it in my pussy first so it had a little moisture on it.

Eventually my ass started lubricating

and loosened up. He snatched the condom off and went into my pussy.

It felt so amazing. My body reacted like I was thrown into a pool of cold water in the winter. Every hair on my body stood up.

"Cum," he said.

Kich came inside of me and I came with him.

I had survived this wasn't too bad.

He pushed my ass out of the air and into the bed.

He then went to get the Don Julio bottle and drank some more. I saw him grab a blind fold and put something else in his pocket. He came back with the bottle in his hand.

He put the blind fold on me and rolled me flat on my stomach.

"This will hurt, but this will remind you," he said.

What will hur....?

"Fuckkkkkkkkkk," I yelled.

Whatever he did stung really bad.

I felt it again.

I tried to bite into the gag as much as I could. I decided I wouldn't be a punk and I would take it.

I held all my cries in. It was over soon.

He took the blindfold off me and I saw him reaching for the Don Julio bottle. He poured it on my back.

I wheezed.

He then walked into the bathroom and came out with a 1st aid kit.

WTF did he do to me?

As he was approaching I saw a razor on the dresser with blood, my blood.

"Come here," he said.

I sat up and scooted over to him.

He pulled out his phone.

"You're officially my property," he said.

He showed me the screen. This nigga had cut his logo into my lower backside where all men grip when they're hitting it from the back. Kich's logo is a K with a M surrounding it that curves around to resemble a rose.

"We will go get it professionally filled in tomorrow, but I wanted to start the process off," he said.

I rested my head on Kich.

"What are your thoughts on it?" he asked.

He removed the gag from my mouth.

"You have permission to speak," he said.

"I love it just as it is. It's already perfect," I said.

Kich went to sit in the chair by the bar.

"Come suck me," he said.

I stood up to walk towards him.

"Crawl," he said.

I paused and got on my knees.

I crawled over to him.

My new homemade tattoo didn't hurt.

Kich put some ointment on it and I could barely feel it. Kich was making sure I could not go back to Lamont. I didn't even have time to think about that elephant in Memphis waiting for me.

I finally made it to Kich and I took his balls in my mouth first. Kich lifted his legs and I already knew what that meant. I stuck my tongue in Kich's ass and began licking from his ass to his balls.

"Yes, Vistoria you're my perfect little slut," he said.

Kich made me so wet whenever he called me degrading names.

I planned to give Kich the best head I could muster up. I would suck his dick all night if he demanded it. I had some major making up to do. Although Kich did plenty to make me pay for my infidelity, a part of me didn't feel like I had done enough.

After I tossed Kich's salad I began sucking him. I deepthroated him and he fucked my face.

Kich came on my face and in my mouth so many times that night. I honestly felt like his fuck toy and that's what I had been missing. There's no way I could go on living a regular life with Lamont. I had no idea how I was going to escape this perilous situation I had gotten myself into.

My bachelorette trip came to a close and it was time to return to Memphis to face reality. These last few days were a dream. So much had changed and I had no idea how I was going to go back as if these things didn't happen.

I woke up in Kich's room the final day of our trip.

"Good morning my seed," Kich said.

"Seed? Umm who are you talking to? Because you have came in me 1000x over these last few days," I said.

"I'm talking about you. You are my seed that makes life grow. We are starseeds from the same planet," he said.

"I like that," I said.

"So how are you going to break it off with your ex-fiance?" Kich asked.

"I'm going to have to see him and talk to him. I owe him that," I said.

"You better be glad I am feeling generous and even allowing you to go back in his presence. I am trying this new thing with you and Mel where I let you make decisions for yourself. I realize we are in this for a lifetime and I can't control every single thing. Honestly, it stresses me out. When I talk with my therapist I do agree that my need for control can be stratospheric," he admitted.

"What? Kich is seeing a therapist?" I said.

"Hey, I'm getting older, better, wiser, and I believe it's time that some of my ghosts get freed," he said.

"I like your ghosts," I kissed him.

"Well there are some that I no longer like. The ones that made me give up on you," he said.

"I put entirely too much pressure on you. The situation with Melanie that I held over her for all these years. I held them because they were comfortable, but I'm ready. You both deserve so much better from me," he said.

"Kich I'm truly loving this," I said.

"So tell me what you decide to do and how you plan to break it to him. I can only imagine how distraught he will be knowing that he's losing you. Let me know if at any moment you feel unsafe," he said.

"I'm gonna think about it on my flight there. This will take some solitude and weighing," I said.

"What is there to weigh? You're saying that as if I'm still an option. I am the choice," he said.

Chapter 15
<u>Choice</u>

So it looks like this is it. Thanks for taking this ride with me. You made it. This is the last chapter. The last part of this series. *sighs*

I've enjoyed this ride with you all. I grew a lot during these years of telling my truth. I hope you get the lessons and I hope you see my truth. My truth isn't what you may want it to be, but it is mine. Being perfect by society's standards is a rip off. But living your life in a way that makes you sincerely happy and pleased regardless of norms...now that's ethereal.

I won't hold you any longer. I am in tears as I write this. Time to see how the story ends. On y va.

<u>Translations of on y va: let's go</u>

My heart was pulsing at an irregular speed and I could feel my palms getting sweaty as I clenched my bouquet tighter.

Oh no, I hope he doesn't have to hold my hand. I'm going to feel icky.

Bitch, that's because you're making a mistake. It's still time to run you haven't even hit the entrance yet. Stop walking now.

Nope, you didn't miss a part of the story. I'm still getting married.

My walking slowed up as I turned left

in the corridor and I could now see all of the white, peach, and yellow roses lining the entrance to the sanctuary.

"Vistoria honey, are you ok?" my dad looked down at me from his tower above.

I looked back up only standing 5 feet and some extra.

"Yes Father, I am fine. I am just a little nervous," I said.

So, that's how you explain talking like a robot just now?

My dad and I weren't the closest but this is what dads do. Dads walk daughters down the aisle even if they are damned.

I bet you can't say that 5x fast.

We made it to the doors and paused before entering. I felt Pearl Harbor getting bombed in that moment. I was on the top floor of the Twin Towers then. My face grew still and cold and I just stared at every crevice in the wooden door before me.

I'm going crazy right here at my wedding. I've literally gone mad.

Run. It's still time.

I can't do that. Can I?

Where would I run?

Are you really about to trap yourself for life all because of some childhood crush?

It's more than a childhood crush. He was there for me when I had no one and I knew nothing. He's part of the reason I turned out to be something at all.

I would've figured it out but you just suppressed me before I could grow. Like now. You're doing it again. He chains you and Kich frees you.

What kind of freedom is that with Kich? Huh? Being number 1 and then number 2? Where will I be with Kich by 40? Number 9?

Where will you be with Lamont by 40? Divorced? None of this is promised that's why you have to live for you. You have to live each day in the present and never stress over the future because in reality only the now exist.

So what does that mean?

In this moment, who do you choose?

When I arrived back in Memphis after the Vegas trip I came clean with Lamont. I told him what had happened on the trip and I was prepared to leave. Unlike Kich who put me out for texting another man Lamont didn't. He forgave me right then and there. He told me he still wanted to marry me, and he knew he would never love anyone as much as me. It was then that I knew no matter what Kich and I had gone through in Vegas it was the end. It was closure. I would dream and think about Kich every moment of my life, but I was here. I was doing this.

But if I was so convinced...why was I sweating tsunamis at my wedding.

And just like that the choice came

hurdling at me again. My eyes were bulging out of my head. I felt betrayed by my body not agreeing with my decision.

Why can't you just choose and live with one fucking choice? Why does it always have to be this complicated?

At this point I was sweating and crying hysterically under my veil.

"Do you take Vistoria Jefferson to be your lawfully wedded wife to have and to hold until death do you part?" Pastor Bryant asked Lamont.

"I do," Lamont replied.

"And Vistoria. Do you take Lamont Ivy to be your lawfully wedded husband to have and to hold until death do you part?" Pastor Bryant asked me.

"I....," I was interrupted by...

Come on now you already know who.

"I object," Kich burst through the door laughing.

"We tried to stop him," security said as my mother jumped up from her seat and rushed to the back of the sanctuary.

"I haven't actually got to that part," Pastor Bryant said.

I looked up at him trying not to smile. *Leave it to Kich to break all the rules. You couldn't even wait to object at the proper part. Asswipe.*

"Get out of here. You are not welcome here," my mom said as she pushed Kich closer to the exit.

"I'm sorry but I believe I need to hear that from your daughter," he said.

"You don't have to hear it from her. She's shown you her answer. Do you not see her at the altar. She's already said "I do" and you are too late," she said.

"There's never a too late in love mam," Kich said.

By now my father had made it to the exit along with my mom.

"Son, I'm going to have to ask you to leave peacefully," he said.

"I'm not leaving unless Vistoria leaves with me," Kich said.

All of Lamont and my guests were looking back and forth from me to Kich.

Kich stood there with his white button

down and black tailored pants. He looked as if he was coming to the wedding as a guest.

"Vistoria! Come with me," Kich yelled from the back.

Lamont looked down at me and I looked up at him.

My heart was crumbling and my lips started to quiver.

"You need to leave now," Lamont yelled from the front.

"You're upsetting my wife on her wedding day," Lamont continued.

"Get out or I will put you out," my dad said to Kich.

"Vistoria, we're leaving now," Kich yelled.

What the fuck are you going to do bitch?

What you gone do hoe?

I can't go now. I can't leave this altar with my family and Lamont's family gawking at me. Lamont is promising to put me first. I can't leave him to be with a man who dates multiple women.

Yeah for now but you don't know the future. He could cheat and it be the equivalent to Kich. The only difference is Kich lays it out up front.

All men don't cheat and that's stupid to think that.

My father by now had started to push

and tussle with Kich.

Kich was laughing as he continued yelling and holding his ground.

"Vistoria, any day now. Bring your ass on," he yelled.

The crowd gasped.

More men got up to go help my father push Kich out the door and that's when it happened. I had learned to live without Lamont. It wasn't easy, but I did it. When I could no longer see Kich because men were now surrounding him I realized I couldn't do it. I could not live without him. And in that instance I hiked up my dress and I ran down the steps of the altar.

"Vistoria, Vistoria baby. What are you doing?" Lamont asked.

My mom saw me coming and tried to block me.

"Vistoria, you get your ass back on that altar now," she said as she grabbed my arm.

"Can it Mom," I said as I snatched away.

I could still hear Kich yelling my name from outside. I didn't look back at Lamont. I couldn't. I should've felt bad for leaving him there, but I didn't. I felt relief. As I got closer to Kich I felt more alive than ever.

Adam and Lilith

*When I first met you
it was like my soul mated with yours.
I would do anything to be in your world.
And I truly believe in a past life
we found a way to make it work.
But in this life....
I must go with the person
my heart wakes and thinks of first.
The one who sets my soul on fire,
my fiber, my twin flame.*

"And that's not you," I said as I kept running.

"Kich!" I yelled.

I disassembled my dress that revealed a tighter, sexier dress for the reception. You know Kara's bibbidi-bobbidi boo ensemble... who by the way was looking at me with complete admiration.

Kich was outside swinging at the air when I made it through the doors.

He looked up at me and instantly stopped swinging and greeted me with open arms.

"Get your ass over here girl," he said as he scooped me up.

"Vistoria, on my soul...don't ever scare me like that again," he said as balmy water breached his face and drenched mine. I felt wetness on my shoulder that was exposed in my reception dress.

I wanted to get far away from that church, but I couldn't interrupt this moment. It was the moment I knew I had been reunited with my twin flame and life partner for good.

He looked at me and opened the passenger side door. I got in.

"I told you. I will hunt you forever," he said as we sped off in his car into the summer day as the crisp wind kissed our cheeks.

And a wedding did happen that day. I vowed to be with Kich forever as he vowed to be with me. We didn't need a pastor to initiate what we knew in our hearts. I also took his last name legally that day. I changed my name to Vistoria Montel. A few years ago if someone had told me I would choose him and I would choose this lifestyle I wouldn't have believed it. But now I couldn't see my life any other way with any other person.

Sincerely,

Vistoria Montel

The End

Questions from fans:

What are Kich's placements?
Kich is a Libra Sun, Scorpio Moon, Capricorn Rising

What is Melanie's sign?
Cancer

What is Vistoria's sign?
Sagittarius

What is Kara's sign?
Aquarius

What is a twinflame?
When one soul is split between two bodies.